# Crypto Hipsters

The Best Guidebook for Beginners in Crypto

## RYAN HAM

PARTRIDGE

**To order additional copies of this book, contact**
Toll Free +65 3165 7531 (Singapore)
Toll Free +60 3 3099 4412 (Malaysia)
orders.singapore@partridgepublishing.com

www.partridgepublishing.com/singapore

# Index

# Introduction

Imagine a world where the notion of digital currency was more than just a speculative whisper among tech enthusiasts—a world on the cusp of financial revolution. It was within this burgeoning digital landscape, on a seemingly ordinary day in May 2010, that a simple transaction for two pizzas would mark one of the most iconic moments in the history of cryptocurrency. This is the story of Bitcoin Pizza Day, an anecdote that beautifully encapsulates the humble beginnings of a movement set to redefine our understanding of money, value, and the mechanisms that govern their exchange.

Laszlo Hanyecz, a programmer and early Bitcoin enthusiast, found himself craving pizza. In a moment of inspiration, he proposed a trade on a Bitcoin forum: 10,000 Bitcoins in exchange for two large pizzas. A fellow forum user took Hanyecz up on his offer, and the deal was struck. At the time, the value of those 10,000 Bitcoins was about $41—a modest sum for two pizzas. Fast forward to today, and the value of those Bitcoins has soared into the millions, making those pizzas the most expensive in history.

This quirky tale is more than just a footnote in cryptocurrency's short but storied existence; it's a testament to the nascent potential of digital currencies and the visionaries who believed in their value before the rest of the world caught on. It signifies the first real-world transaction using Bitcoin, setting the stage for the myriad ways in which this new form of money could be used.

But why start our journey into the world of cryptocurrency with this story? Because it perfectly illustrates the journey of cryptocurrency itself—from an obscure, experimental form of digital cash to a global financial phenomenon. This book is written for those curious souls standing at the threshold of this new digital frontier, looking to understand not just the how and the what, but the why of cryptocurrency.

Our exploration begins at the very foundation, with the blockchain technology that underpins cryptocurrencies like Bitcoin. Understanding blockchain is essential, for it is the heart of the cryptocurrency revolution—a decentralized ledger that promises security, transparency, and efficiency.

As we delve deeper, we'll navigate through the intricacies of various cryptocurrencies, demystifying how they work, why they hold value, and how you can engage with them safely and effectively. This book aims to equip you with the knowledge to confidently participate in cryptocurrency discussions, investments, and applications.

Moreover, we will look into the potential of cryptocurrencies to alter the financial landscape. Then, examine the economic and philosophical implications of a decentralized currency, pondering its ability to challenge and potentially upend traditional banking systems.

Moreover, this book addresses the inevitable challenges and risks that accompany any groundbreaking innovation. From the volatility of cryptocurrency markets to the evolving regulatory landscape, understanding these hurdles is crucial for anyone venturing into this space.

But the journey doesn't end with investment and speculation. We're on the brink of a broader technological revolution, with blockchain poised to transform industries beyond finance. Through discussions on smart contracts, decentralized finance (DeFi), non-fungible tokens (NFTs), and more, we'll explore the far-reaching implications of this technology.

This book is your gateway to the world of cryptocurrency. Whether you're drawn to the investment potential of digital currencies, intrigued by the technology behind them, or simply curious about the future of finance, my aim is to provide a comprehensive and accessible guide to the crypto universe.

So, why read this book? Because understanding cryptocurrency today is akin to understanding the internet in the early '90s. It's a chance to be at the forefront of a technological paradigm shift, armed with the knowledge and insight to navigate its opportunities and challenges. Join this journey with me and welcome to the future of money.

# Chapter 1

# Unveiling the Money

## Money like Chameleon

*$100 dollar backed by the U.S. government as a legal tender*

Let's stare at this $100 bill. What makes you feel? You might imagine getting a stack of $100 bills for your outstanding work for a bonus, or perhaps you are thinking about the dollar printing machine underneath the dark basement of the Bureau of Engraving and Printing. Perhaps you might be imagining hanging out with your friends in a club with a dollar shooting gun.

Money is a mysterious existence. We laugh and cry because of money, sometimes craving so badly but sometimes neglecting and shouting out "Happiness does not come from money". However, there is no argument that it is the driving force of what makes us wake up early every morning with our sleepy eyes and go to work with a cup of coffee.

We use money all the time, it is like the breathing air of our society. Money is spent from buying a cup of coffee, fueling our car and paying our rent. But did you ever take it seriously about the core existence of the money? How it was first started, where it is made, how the quantity is maintained.

Bitcoin and blockchain technology was first created to replace the throne of fiat currency, so it is necessary to understand the characteristics of money in advance.

Let's take a look at the history of money from the beginning to the present. You are going to learn that the money we are using right now is not just granted. Also it would be interesting to see how the money's appearance had changed by the evolution of society. The range encompasses from Barter system(Prehistoric times), Commodity Money(3000-1000 BC), Metal Money and Coinage (around 1000 BC), Paper Money($7^{th}$ Century AD), Gold Standard($19^{th}$ Century), Fiat Money($20^{th}$ Century onwards) to Electronic Money and Digital Currencies(Current).

## Barter System (Prehistoric times)

The barter system represents an early form of economic exchange where goods and services were directly traded without the intermediary use of money. Central to this system was the principle of direct exchange, fulfilling immediate needs through mutual negotiation. Each party in a barter transaction had to possess something the other desired, making the process highly dependent on individual requirements and the perceived value of the items or services offered. The absence of a standard unit of value meant that the worth of exchanged goods was subjective and varied according to each trade.

However, the barter system faced notable challenges. The most significant was the need for a double coincidence of wants, requiring both parties in a trade to have what the other wanted. This requirement often made it difficult to find suitable trading partners. Additionally, issues such as the indivisibility of certain goods (like livestock) and the perishability of items like food products limited the practicality of barter. These limitations were particularly pronounced when attempting to store wealth or conduct trades over larger distances or longer periods, as the system lacked a reliable means of preserving or transporting value efficiently. Despite these challenges, barter served as a foundational economic practice in many early societies, especially in small communities or in times when currency was scarce.

## Commodity Money (3000-1000 BC)

Commodity money marks a pivotal stage in the history of money, characterized by the use of items with intrinsic value as a medium of exchange. Unlike barter, where goods and services were directly exchanged, commodity money involved commodities that were universally valued for their utility and rarity. Common examples include gold, silver, salt, cattle, and grains. These commodities were chosen for their durability, divisibility, portability, and widespread desirability. This evolution from barter to commodity money was significant because it circumvented the need for a double coincidence of wants, a major limitation of bartering.

Precious metals like gold and silver were universally valued commodities and formed the basis of early coinage in civilizations such as ancient Egypt, Greece, and Rome, with the Roman denarius being a notable example. Salt, crucial for food preservation, also served as commodity money; its historical importance is reflected in the term "salary," originating from the Roman practice of compensating soldiers with salt. Similarly, cattle, vital in agrarian societies, were used as a standard form of payment in places like ancient Ireland. In various cultures across Africa, Asia, and North America, shells, particularly cowries, became a medium of exchange due to their rarity and aesthetic appeal. In agrarian economies like ancient Egypt and Mesopotamia, grains, a staple food, were used as money, while in regions like Central Asia, tea bricks, essential for their nutritional value, served a similar purpose.

The shift to commodity money brought several advantages and marked a leap forward in economic systems. It facilitated easier storage of value, overcoming the perishability and bulkiness of many barter goods. It also enabled long-distance trade, which was previously impractical with barter. Furthermore, the divisibility of commodities, particularly metals, allowed for transactions of varying sizes. Despite these benefits, commodity money had its limitations. The supply of these commodities could be unpredictable, affected by factors like new discoveries, technological changes, or trade routes, leading to fluctuations in value. Additionally, the physical nature of commodity money, especially heavier items like metals, posed challenges in terms of transportation and security in large quantities. These limitations notwithstanding, commodity money represented a significant advancement in the understanding and practice of trade and economics, laying groundwork for more sophisticated economic transactions.

## Metal Money and Coinage (around 1000 BC)

Metal money and coinage, emerging around 600 BC in Lydia with the creation of electrum coins, marked a significant advancement in the history of money. This innovation quickly spread to ancient Greece and Rome, with civilizations adopting standardized silver and gold coins, enhancing trade efficiency across the Mediterranean. Metal coinage offered numerous advantages over earlier forms of money, such as durability, portability, divisibility, and standardized values. The intrinsic value of metals like gold, silver, and bronze provided a stable and widely accepted basis for transactions, facilitating trade over vast distances and between diverse cultures.

The introduction of coinage profoundly impacted both economies and societies. It enabled the development of more complex trade networks, markets, cities, and even contributed to the expansion of empires by streamlining tax collection and army payments. Coins also held cultural significance, often bearing the images of rulers or deities, reflecting the state's power and religious beliefs. Notable examples include the Roman denarius, known for its silver content, and the various forms of bronze coinage in China during the Zhou dynasty, which evolved into round coins with square holes.

This transition to metal money and coinage represented a pivotal moment in economic history, laying the groundwork for modern financial systems. By providing a reliable and convenient medium for transactions, metal coins were instrumental in the evolution from primitive trade practices to more sophisticated economic structures.

# Paper Money (7ᵗʰ Century AD)

Paper money, began in China during the Tang Dynasty (618-907 AD). Initially emerging as promissory notes to ease the burden of transporting copper coins, it evolved into government-issued currency, known as "Jiaozi" during the Song Dynasty. This innovation responded to the need for a more efficient medium of exchange amidst a growing economy and copper shortages. The concept was later documented by Marco Polo during the Yuan Dynasty, highlighting its widespread acceptance in China.

The adoption of paper money in Europe occurred significantly later, with the first European banknotes issued in the 1660s by Stockholms Banco in Sweden. These early notes were essentially receipts for coin deposits. In the Americas, the Massachusetts Bay Colony was a pioneer, issuing paper money in 1690 to fund military efforts. Over the 17ᵗʰ and 18ᵗʰ centuries, paper money became more common in Europe and the American colonies, transitioning from being a representative note, backed by commodities like gold or silver, to fiat money, which holds value based on government decree and public trust.

This shift to paper money marked a major shift from commodity-based currencies to a more abstract value system. It allowed for greater flexibility in controlling money supplies and facilitated the expansion of larger-scale economies and international trade. Today's paper currency, predominantly fiat money, is equipped with advanced security features to prevent counterfeiting, reflecting ongoing innovations in the field of monetary systems.

# Gold Standard (19ᵗʰ Century)

The gold standard was a monetary system where a country's currency had its value directly linked to gold, widely adopted in the 19ᵗʰ century, with the United Kingdom formalizing its use in 1821. Under this system, currencies were convertible into gold at a fixed rate, and the value of different currencies was determined by their gold content, facilitating stable and predictable international trade. For instance, the British pound sterling was defined in terms of a specific weight of gold. The primary advantage of the gold standard was its ability to control inflation by limiting the money supply to the amount of gold a nation held. However, this also restricted government flexibility in monetary policy, especially during economic downturns, potentially leading to deflation and exacerbating economic issues.

The United States adopted the gold standard in 1879, and many other countries followed, leading to what is known as the classical gold standard era. However, the outbreak of World War I saw many countries abandon the gold standard to print more money for war financing. Attempts to return to the gold standard post-WWI were unstable and ultimately collapsed during the Great Depression. The U.S. officially moved away from the gold standard in 1933, and the complete abandonment of this system by most countries was marked by the collapse of the Bretton Woods system in 1971.

This shift away from the gold standard marked a significant transition in global financial systems, from a rigid, gold-based monetary policy to more flexible fiat money systems. The end of the gold standard allowed governments greater control over their economic policies and the ability to adjust their money supply based on prevailing economic conditions, rather than being constrained by the physical availability of gold.

Abolition of the gold standard is a pretty important event in modern history of money. It's also closely linked to the birth of Bitcoin too. We will delve deeper into this topic in further.

## Fiat Money (20th Century onwards)

Fiat money is a type of currency that derives its value not from any intrinsic worth or convertibility into a commodity, but from the trust and authority of the government that issues it. The term "fiat" originates from Latin, meaning "let it be done," indicating that the currency's value is established by government decree. Unlike commodity-based or representative currencies, fiat money, which includes most modern paper currencies and coins, has no intrinsic value. Its value and stability are contingent upon the public's confidence in the issuing government and its ability to maintain a stable economy.

The use of fiat money has occurred sporadically throughout history, with one of the earliest examples in 11th-century China, during the Song Dynasty. However, the widespread adoption of fiat money as the dominant form of currency is a 20th-century development. This shift was largely due to the abandonment of the gold standard, particularly after the Bretton Woods Agreement in 1944 and its collapse in 1971. Most national currencies today, including the US dollar, the Euro, and the Korean Won, are examples of fiat money.

The transition to fiat money marked a significant evolution in monetary systems, allowing governments greater control over economic policies. It enabled them to effectively manage the money supply and respond to economic challenges like inflation or deflation. However, this shift also introduced risks such as potential mismanagement, which could lead to issues like hyperinflation, underscoring the importance of responsible monetary governance.

## Electronic Money and Digital Currencies (Current)

The current electronic money system is a sophisticated network that facilitates digital monetary transactions, integrating various technologies and financial instruments. Key components include digital transactions that enable the electronic transfer of funds between accounts, online banking which offers customers the ability to manage their finances over the internet, and mobile payments and wallets, where smartphones are used for secure, contactless payments. Credit and debit cards continue to play a vital role, linking users to their bank accounts or credit lines for both physical and online transactions.

Furthermore, peer-to-peer (P2P) payment systems like PayPal and Venmo have simplified direct money transfers between individuals, often requiring only an email address or phone number. The rise of e-commerce platforms has further entrenched electronic money's role in daily transactions, allowing for seamless digital payments. Automated Clearing Houses (ACH) networks are also crucial, processing large volumes of transactions such as direct deposits and payroll efficiently. While offering convenience and efficiency, this system necessitates robust cybersecurity measures to safeguard against fraud and ensure inclusive access amidst the digital divide.

# 4 key events

We have just swiftly gone through the history of money. What have you felt about it? You might have guessed that money had come a long way in history from the beginning of our civilization and also transformed its outlooks in many different ways. And you should have felt something awkward about the last part of the stage which is the "Fiat Money".

Let's read carefully about the characteristics of fiat money.

*"No intrinsic value but is declared as a legal tender by a government"*

While thinking about this sentence, let's dive into the four most significant issues that happened in the 20th and 21th century.

## 1. Gold standard of dollar and it's abolition

Why do you think that people in the globe first used the dollar as a global currency in the first place? It is closely related to the "Gold standard" of the dollar.

The gold standard of the U.S. dollar was a monetary system in which the value of the dollar was directly tied to a specific quantity of gold. Under the gold standard, the U.S. government guaranteed that it would redeem any amount of dollars for its equivalent value in gold. This system provided stability to currency values, limiting inflation and promoting confidence in the currency.

The US dollar supremacy started at the end of the Second World War. There was literally no functioning global economy, so nations got together to create a new trading system and a new monetary system. That monetary system was devised in a town in New Hampshire called Bretton Woods, so it was called the Bretton Woods Agreement. One of the key elements was that the dollar would be pegged to gold at $35 an ounce. Other central banks could exchange the dollars they held for gold. In that sense, the dollar was as good as gold. Every other currency had a fixed exchange rate to the dollar.

They established the dollar-gold standard to create some predictability and stability for global commerce. For the next 25 years, it was a tremendous success. The dollar became the global currency. Everyone was happy to hold it, in large part because they could exchange it for gold if they had any doubts about its value. It was part of the phenomenal recovery from the war in Europe and Japan. It also created enormous economic prosperity in the U.S., all through the '50s and '60s.

When the Nixon administration came into office in 1969, they realized that the world economy had grown very, very big. Everybody wanted dollars, so the Federal Reserve was printing lots of dollars. As a result, there were four times as many dollars in circulation as there was gold in reserves.

The rate of $35 for an ounce of gold was good in 1944, but it hadn't changed, so by 1971 the dollar was really overvalued. That meant imports were very cheap, and exports were very expensive. The U.S. experienced its first trade deficit since the 19th century and was experiencing employment problems. For the first time, the U.S. started to talk about losing competitiveness.

In the broadest sense, the United States couldn't uphold all of the responsibilities that it inherited after the Second World War. For decades, the U.S. was so predominant that we could help everybody; we lifted the world economy and didn't worry about the domestic economy because it was so strong. Nineteen seventy-one was the year the U.S. began to understand the Marshall Plan mentality was over.

On top of all that, there was the beginning of inflation. If it continued long enough, dollars would be worth less than they were before. The Nixon Administration was afraid that other countries were going to ask for gold and the U.S. wouldn't have it. That would have been an enormous humiliation and a breaking of their commitment to exchange gold for dollars.

What the U.S. really wanted was some way to devalue the dollar, but because it was pegged to gold, the administration couldn't do that. In 1971, then-U.S. President Richard Nixon announced the suspension of the dollar's convertibility to gold. This decision, known as the "Nixon Shock," marked the end of the Bretton Woods system and the abandonment of the gold standard for the U.S. dollar.

As a result of the suspension, the value of the U.S. dollar was no longer directly tied to a fixed quantity of gold, allowing it to float in the foreign exchange markets.

## 2. 2008 financial crisis and subprime mortgage

Those who were born before 1990 and were doing their social activity in 2008 could not forget the nightmare of the financial crisis that happened in that year. Millions of individuals faced job losses, and numerous banks, including the renowned Lehman Brothers, declared bankruptcy during the widespread economic downturn. The term "Subprime mortgage" may sound familiar to you, as it served as the primary catalyst for this catastrophic event.

## U.S. economic stimulus package after the Great Depression of 1938

To expand housing supply and stimulate the economy, the Roosevelt administration created a government agency called Fannie Mae, which provided funds to banks by purchasing government-guaranteed mortgage loan assets from them.

Banks that were in a state of a credit crunch were able to transfer the risk of mortgage loans to the government, and were also able to make new mortgage loans using the proceeds from the sale of mortgage assets.

When privatizing Fannie Mae in 1968, the U.S. Congress established Ginnie Mae, a state-run corporation that guaranteed mortgage-related bonds, and Ginnie Mae provided guarantees for the first MBS. MBS, stands for Mortgage Backed Securities, is a new bond using a pool of mortgage assets as collateral and sells them to investors, transferring the principal and interest generated from the mortgage pool to investors.

Thanks to MBS, banks were able to make new mortgage loans by securitizing mortgage assets, which were sold to investors not only in the United States but also around the world, playing a role in sucking funds from around the world into the U.S. real estate market.

## Growth of the mortgage market in the 1990s

In the 1990s, the Democratic Clinton administration made raising the housing supply rate, which was only 65% during the Republican Reagon administration, a major policy goal during its term. In particular, policies were implemented to expand housing supply to low-income groups where subprime and deep-subprime classes were located.

However, large banks such as Fannie Mae and Frddie Mac did not actively participate in the high-risk subprime market because they were already reaping large profits from the prime mortgage business alone.

| Credit Score Types | |
|---|---|
| Superprime | 781-850 |
| Prime | 661-780 |
| Nonprime | 601-660 |
| Subprime | 501-600 |
| Deep Subprime | 300-500 |

*Backed by Monoline, people who were below the Subprime class could lend money to buy houses.*

Ultimately, the subprime mortgage market was dominated by professional mortgage companies through aggressive marketing backed by the guarantee of Monoline, an MBS bond guarantee agency.

As the subprime mortgage market became active, housing demand increased throughout the 1990s, and housing prices continued to rise. Thanks to the booming housing economy, subprime mortgage companies reaped large profits, and large banks that had been focusing on the prime market also entered the subprime mortgage market to avoid fierce competition in the prime market.

In 1998, the size of subprime mortgage loans reached $145 billion, showing a growth of more than 400% compared to five years ago.

## Complex derivatives underlined by MBS

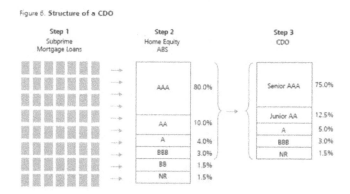

Figure 6. Structure of a CDO

*MBS from different credit classes were mixed, creating a new CDO. Source: NERA economic consulting*

In the mortgage market, derivative financial products, including MBS, have evolved into more complex forms. In the case of CDO (Collateralized Debt Obligation), a pool is created by combining MBS and various other bonds, and then this pool is divided into several tranches with different priorities and issued as collateral.

Because it is very difficult to evaluate the risk of these complex bonds, investors rely on credit ratings published by credit rating agencies to evaluate the risk of bonds. However, from the credit rating agency's perspective, since the bond issuer is the customer, a structural collusion relationship has occurred between the bond issuer and the credit rating agency, leading to cases where bond issuing companies engage in 'rate shopping.' In the end, the early warning function of credit rating companies for bad bonds was neutralized, laying the seeds for a financial crisis.

## Rise of an interest rate and the deadly catastrophe

The U.S. Federal Reserve began raising the base interest rate at the end of June 2004, rising to 5.25% at the end of June 2006, and then remaining fixed for a while. As the base interest rate rose, the mortgage interest rate also rose, and the mortgage delinquency rate began to increase accordingly. This is because many of those who received subprime mortgage loans received loans with variable interest rates.

As the demand for mortgage loans decreased due to rising interest rates and delinquency rates increased, the value of MBS bonds began to fall in the bond market, and accordingly, banks sold risky assets to the market to fulfill their obligations to maintain BIS Capital Adequacy Ratio.

Because most financial institutions were in a similar situation, the market was flooded with supply, causing a further decline in mortgage bond prices. In addition, as the issuance of mortgage bonds becomes difficult and mortgage lending is blocked, the following vicious cycle occurs.

Decrease in housing demand => Fall in real estate prices => Fall in the bank's asset value => Bank's valuation loss => Each bank sells mortgage bonds again to meet the BIS ratio => Fall in bond price => Fall in the bank's asset value and so on. The U.S. housing market was falling to an endless swirl.

Eventually, the U.S. government had to intervene to stop this disaster. Fannie Mae and Freddie Mac were nationalized and Merril Lynch was sold to Bank of America. Morgan Stanley and Goldman Sachs gave up remaining as independent investment banks and converted into bank holding companies with commercial banks as subsidiaries.

# Bail out

To overcome the financial crisis caused by the subprime mortgage, central banks in major countries such as the United States and the United Kingdom provided bailout loans to large financial companies such as AIG.

Afterwards, market bonds such as mortgage-backed bonds were purchased through the quantitative easing policy of issuing currency to stimulate the economy.

This policy exempts those responsible for economic failure from financial, regulatory, or criminal punishment, and shifts the burden of inflation, the gap between rich and poor due to rising asset prices, and unemployment problems on taxpayers.

# 3. Quantitative Easing

Quantitative easing(QE) is one of the magical powers that makes dollars so strong. If the term sounds a little bit intimidating, you can simply just remember this term as "QE = creating dollars from thin air". It is a non-traditional monetary policy tool used by central banks, including the Federal Reserve in the United States, to stimulate the economy when standard monetary policy measures, such as adjusting interest rates, become less effective.

Through QE, central banks create new money electronically to buy government bonds or other financial assets from banks or financial institutions. This process increases the money supply and reduces long-term interest rates by raising bond prices and lowering their yields. The core idea is to encourage banks to increase lending to consumers and businesses, thereby boosting investment and consumption.

One of the most prominent examples of QE was implemented by the U.S. Federal Reserve during the 2008 financial crisis. After reducing its benchmark interest rate to nearly zero, the Fed embarked on several rounds of QE, buying substantial amounts of government securities and mortgage-backed securities. This action was intended to provide liquidity, stabilize the financial system, and support economic recovery. Similarly, the European Central Bank (ECB) initiated QE in 2015 in response to the Eurozone debt crisis and deflationary risks. The ECB's asset purchases were aimed at lowering interest rates and boosting inflation towards their target rate.

## QE workflow

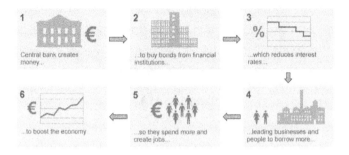

*QE happens in these sequential steps. Source: BBC*

- **Asset Purchases:** The Federal Reserve buys financial assets from the open market, typically long-term government securities such as Treasury bonds and sometimes other securities like mortgage-backed securities.

- **Increasing Reserves:** Sellers of these assets, which are often financial institutions, receive payment from the Federal Reserve. This injection of money into the financial system increases the reserves held by banks.

- **Lowering Long-Term Interest Rates:** By purchasing long-term securities, the Fed aims to lower long-term interest rates. This is intended to encourage borrowing and spending by both consumers and businesses.

- **Stimulating Economic Activity:** The primary goal of quantitative easing is to stimulate economic activity. Lowering interest rates makes borrowing cheaper, encourages spending and investment, and helps prevent deflationary pressures.

There are some new terminologies coming out such as "long-term securities" and "interest rate". Don't worry, let's take it slow. Long-term securities refer to financial instruments or assets with an extended maturity period. These can include bonds, stocks, and other investment vehicles that have a significant duration before reaching maturity or being redeemed.

Interest rates represent the cost of borrowing money or the return on investment for lending or holding money. They are expressed as a percentage of the principal amount. Interest rates are a crucial factor in financial markets. Central banks, such as the Federal Reserve in the United States, often set short-term interest rates as part of their monetary policy to influence economic conditions, inflation, and employment.

## 2008 QE vs 2020 QE

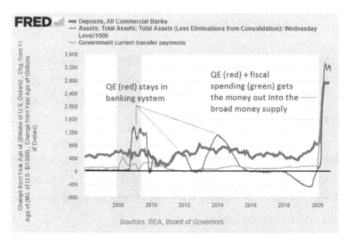

*2008 was a year when QE first happened. In 2020, FED released tremendous amount of money*

The application of Quantitative Easing (QE) during the 2008 financial crisis and the 2020 coronavirus pandemic presented notable differences in execution and impact on the economy, particularly in the United States. In the 2008-2014 period, despite significant QE as indicated by the rising red line in your chart, there was minimal increase in public bank deposits, which form a large part of the broad money supply. This was primarily because the QE efforts largely focused on recapitalizing banks without a direct fiscal transmission mechanism to the broader economy. Government transfer payments and bank deposits, represented by the green and blue lines respectively, remained relatively low, indicating that the QE did not significantly boost personal income or net worth at a national level.

In stark contrast, the response to the 2020 crisis involved not just substantial QE but also direct fiscal interventions, resulting in a dramatic increase in government transfer payments and bank deposits. The U.S. government issued large financial aids directly to people and businesses, significantly financed through the issuance of Treasury bonds. The Federal Reserve, in turn, created new bank reserves to purchase these bonds, primarily in the secondary market. This direct injection of funds led to a sharp rise in personal income and net worth, as shown by the vertical surge in the blue (bank deposits), green (government transfer payments), and red (QE) lines in your chart. Unlike in 2008, the QE process in 2020 was complemented by substantial fiscal support, effectively increasing the money supply in the hands of the public and businesses.

## Potential danger of QE

Quantitative easing (QE), while a potent tool for stimulating economic activity in times of low interest rates, harbors several risks. Firstly, inflation is a prominent concern. QE increases the money supply, which can devalue the currency and lead to higher prices for goods and services if not matched by corresponding economic growth. Additionally, it can inflate asset prices, creating bubbles in markets like real estate and stocks. These bubbles pose a risk of severe financial crises when they burst. QE may also contribute to income inequality, as it disproportionately benefits those who own assets that rise in value, typically the wealthier segment of society, while the less affluent, with minimal asset holdings, gain little.

Furthermore, over-reliance on QE can diminish the effectiveness of traditional monetary policy tools, leading to challenges in steering the economy using conventional methods. This reliance can also result in currency devaluation, making imports more expensive and potentially increasing the cost of living. The increased money supply and low interest rates can encourage governments to accumulate higher levels of debt, potentially leading to sustainability issues. Lastly, unwinding QE poses its own set of challenges, as central banks must navigate the complex process of reducing their asset holdings and increasing interest rates without triggering market volatility or economic instability. These factors make the exit strategy from QE as critical as its implementation, demanding careful consideration and management to avoid negative economic repercussions.

## 4. Hyperinflation

Hyperinflation is an economic condition characterized by an extremely high and rapidly increasing rate of inflation, often exceeding hundreds of percent per year. It leads to a severe devaluation of currency and is generally caused by a significant increase in the money supply that isn't supported by growth in the country's gross domestic product. Hyperinflation results in a drastic drop in the purchasing power of money, rendering it virtually worthless.

*A German woman lights up a fire with worthless banknotes, 1923 / Hyperinflation in Zimbabwe 2008-2009*

One of the most notable instances of hyperinflation occurred in Germany in the 1920s, following World War I. The German government, burdened by heavy war reparations and economic instability, resorted to printing more money, which led to the rapid devaluation of the German Mark. During its peak in 1923, prices were doubling every few days. This economic turmoil significantly contributed to social unrest and the eventual rise of the Nazi Party. Another extreme case was witnessed in Zimbabwe in the late 2000s, where the government's policy of land redistribution and subsequent agricultural collapse led to the printing of more money, resulting in an astronomical inflation rate of 79.6 billion percent month-on-month by late 2008. This hyperinflation led to severe poverty, a breakdown of the financial system, and the abandonment of the Zimbabwean dollar.

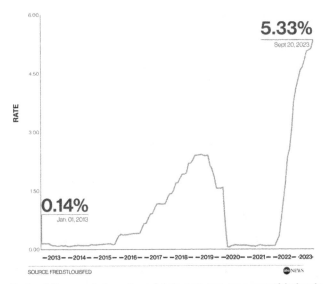

*Federal Reserve's benchmark interest rate on a monthly basis*

How does "Hyperinflation" relate to QE? The fastest way to make currency devaluation is printing money insanely. This is why Jerome Powell, the head of FED is so obsessed with increasing interest rates to adjust the inflation rate now. Due to the low interest rate and tons of dollars created by QE released during Covid-19.

By raising interest rates, the Fed seeks to reduce inflationary pressures by cooling economic activity, aligning with its mandate to achieve stable prices and maximum employment. This approach might also be complemented by quantitative tightening, the opposite concept of quantitative easing, which involves reducing the Fed's balance sheet and further contracting the money supply.

Higher interest rates lead to more expensive borrowing costs, potentially slowing down consumer spending and business investments. While this strategy aims to control inflation, it carries the inherent risk of triggering a recession if implemented too aggressively. The Fed, particularly under the leadership of figures like Jerome Powell, monitors economic indicators closely to adjust its policy and achieve a "soft landing" – effectively controlling inflation without causing a major economic slowdown. The impact of these measures extends beyond U.S. borders, affecting global markets and exchange rates, underscoring the global influence of U.S. monetary policy.

## Cypherpunk movements

*May/June 1993 cover of Wired. Source: Wired*

The Cypherpunk movement, emerging in the late 1980s and early 1990s, is rooted in libertarian and anarchist ideologies, advocating for the use of strong cryptography and privacy-enhancing technologies as tools for social and political change. Influential figures such as David Chaum, Timothy C. May, Eric Hughes, and John Gilmore played pivotal roles in its development, with Chaum's seminal paper on secure digital communication laying the foundational philosophy. The movement gained momentum through the Cypherpunk mailing list, which became a crucial forum for discussions on privacy, cryptography, and related political issues.

Central to the Cypherpunk ethos is the emphasis on individual privacy and anonymity, advocating for public access to strong cryptography as a means to protect against government and corporate surveillance. This philosophy is marked by a deep-seated skepticism of centralized authority, promoting decentralization and individual autonomy. Cypherpunks have significantly contributed to the development of technologies geared towards encryption and privacy, such as Pretty Good Privacy (PGP), and have influenced the genesis and growth of blockchain technology and cryptocurrencies, with Bitcoin being a notable example.

The legacy of the Cypherpunk movement extends far beyond its initial conception, continuing to influence modern technologies and digital rights movements. Its principles of privacy, security, and freedom are more relevant than ever in today's digital landscape, shaping the development and ethos of current blockchain and cryptocurrency projects. Despite facing criticism for the potential misuse of anonymous technologies, the movement's impact on fostering a more secure and private digital world is undeniable, underscoring the balance between privacy rights and societal responsibilities.

## Cypherpunks' philosophy

- **Privacy Advocacy**: Cypherpunks strongly believe in the right to privacy and view it as a fundamental human right. They advocate for the use of cryptographic tools to secure personal communications and data, aiming to protect individuals from unwarranted surveillance.

- **Cryptography as Empowerment**: The Cypherpunk movement sees strong cryptography as a tool that empowers individuals. By using encryption technologies, individuals can control access to their information, communicate privately, and resist unwarranted intrusion into their lives.

- **Decentralization**: Cypherpunks often favor decentralized technologies that distribute power and control. They are wary of centralized authorities, including governments and large corporations, and seek to promote systems that allow individuals to maintain greater autonomy.

- **Open Source Philosophy**: Many Cypherpunks support the open source software movement. Open source principles, which involve making source code freely available for inspection and modification, align with the Cypherpunk ethos of transparency and trust.

- **Resistance to Surveillance**: Cypherpunks resist and challenge mass surveillance. They believe that widespread surveillance poses a threat to civil liberties and can be used for nefarious purposes, emphasizing the need to protect individual privacy in the face of technological advancements.

- **Pseudonymity and Anonymity**: The use of pseudonyms and efforts to maintain online anonymity are common practices among Cypherpunks. This reflects a desire to shield one's identity from surveillance and protect individuals from potential repercussions for their views and activities.

- **Political Activism**: The Cypherpunk movement is not just about technology; it also involves political activism. Adherents seek to raise awareness about privacy issues, advocate for policy changes that protect individual rights, and engage in discussions about the societal implications of technological developments.

## Preceding Cypherpunks movements before Bitcoin

Bitcoin and blockchain technology are integral components of the ethos of the Cypherpunk movement. It did not come out of the thin air! These projects listed in below table are the preceding endeavors aimed at aligning the monetary system with the principles of the Cypherpunk movement that predate the emergence of Bitcoin.

| Year | Name | Description |
|------|------|-------------|
| 1990 | DigiCash | Developed by David Chaum, DigiCash was an electronic cash system that provided secure and private digital transactions, pioneering concepts in digital privacy. |
| 1990s | Mondex | A smart card-based electronic cash system introduced in the 1990s, allowing offline transactions. It aimed to provide a secure and efficient means of digital payments. |
| 1994 | CyberCash | This company developed electronic payment systems, including digital wallets and electronic checks, to enable secure online transactions. |
| 1996 | E-gold | An innovative digital gold currency that allowed users to conduct online payments backed by physical gold, offering an alternative to traditional currency. |
| 1997 | Hashcash | Proposed by Adam Back, Hashcash was a proof-of-work system designed to counter email spam and denial-of-service attacks, requiring computational effort for sending emails. |
| 1998 | Bit Gold | Nick Szabo's proposal for a decentralized digital currency system, Bit Gold included elements that were later incorporated into modern cryptocurrency designs. |

| 1998 | B-Money | Proposed by Wei Dai, B-Money was a concept for a decentralized digital currency system emphasizing cryptographic protocols for creating and transferring money. |
| --- | --- | --- |
| - | Lucre | A digital cash proposal by Cypherpunk Tim May, Lucre focused on cryptographic techniques to enhance anonymity in electronic transactions. |

# Chapter 2

# Bitcoin and Blockchain fundamentals

The journey of money, from barter systems to gold coins, and from paper currency to digital transactions as we have seen in Chapter 1 has been a cornerstone of human civilization's evolution. In Chapter 2, we will look at the emergence of Bitcoin and blockchain technology, which marks a pivotal moment, redefining our understanding of what currency can be in the digital era. Introduced in 2008 by an entity known as Satoshi Nakamoto, Bitcoin is not just another step in the evolution of money – it's a paradigm shift, a decentralized digital currency that operates independently of a central authority.

Bitcoin's emergence can be seen as a response to the growing need for autonomy and transparency in financial transactions, especially in the wake of the 2008 financial crisis. This innovative digital currency operates on a peer-to-peer network, free from the control of governments and financial institutions, thereby democratizing the financial landscape.

The backbone of Bitcoin, blockchain, is a technological marvel in its own right. Blockchain is a distributed ledger that records transactions across many computers so that the record cannot be altered retroactively. This technology, which extends far beyond the realm of cryptocurrencies, offers a new level of security and transparency in digital transactions. It represents not just a technological advancement, but a rethinking of trust and security in a digital world.

As we delve into the world of Bitcoin and explore the intricacies of blockchain, we are not just learning about a new type of currency or a novel tech phenomenon. We are witnessing a historic moment in the long story of money – a moment that challenges the traditional financial systems and opens up a world of possibilities for secure, decentralized transactions.

# 4 concepts in advance

I know all of you are eager to dive right into how all this blockchain works under the hood. However, there are some key concepts we should know in advance. Their existences are "Bit & Byte", "Hash function", "Asymmetric key cryptography" and "Merkle tree". Let's dissect them one by one.

## 1. Bit & Byte

In computer science, a bit is the fundamental unit of data, represented as either 0 or 1. It signifies the binary state of digital information, forming the basis of all data processing and storage in computers. Bits are crucial for encoding everything from simple binary operations to complex data structures and instructions in digital systems.

A byte, typically comprising eight bits, is a more practical unit for handling data. It's used to encode a single character, such as a letter or symbol, especially in text encoding standards like ASCII. Bytes and their multiples (kilobytes, megabytes, gigabytes, etc.) are standard units for measuring file sizes and data transfer rates in computing. Together, bits and bytes represent and process the vast quantities of digital data in computer systems, with bytes offering a more efficient means of data representation and measurement for practical applications.

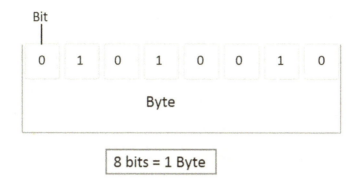

*8 digits of bits making one byte.*

## 2. Hash function

*"Hashed" means to hack or chop, like potatoes are
hashed to make this delicious food!*

What is your favorite potato food? Personally, my pick is hash brown! It gives a more rich texture and crispy taste, oh it's making me hungry just by imagining it. The word hash in here means "to chop into small pieces". And surprisingly, this hash is also used in blockchain technology.

Let's first look how the hash is used in blockchain. There is a specific function which does "hash" and it is called the "hash function".

A hash function is a mathematical function that takes an input (or 'message') and produces a fixed-size string of characters, which is typically a hash value or digest. The primary purpose of a hash function is to uniquely represent data of arbitrary size in a fixed-size format. Hash functions are commonly used in various computer science applications, such as data integrity verification, password storage, digital signatures, and hash tables.

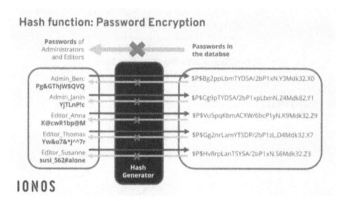

*The hash function in the picture, all of the different passwords are converted into fixed-length strings before being stored in the database. These output strings cannot be converted back to find out the actual password.*

The key characteristic of a hash function is that it is deterministic with the same input, random output with its input value and hard to determine the pre-image value with its output. These are some additional characteristics of a hash function good to know about.

- **Deterministic**: For the same input, a hash function will always produce the same output. This property ensures consistency and predictability.

- **Fixed Output Size**: Regardless of the size or length of the input data, the hash function generates a fixed-size hash value. This allows for efficient storage and comparison of hash values.

- **Efficient Computation**: Hash functions are designed to be computationally efficient, enabling quick calculation of the hash value for any given input.

- **Irreversibility (One-Way Function)**: It should be computationally infeasible to reverse the hash function and obtain the original input from its hash value. This property is essential for security applications, such as password storage, where it is desirable to protect user passwords.

- **Avalanche Effect**: A small change in the input should result in a significantly different hash value. This property ensures that similar inputs do not produce similar hash values, enhancing the security and reliability of the hash function.

- **Pre-image Resistance**: Given a hash value, it should be computationally infeasible to find any input that produces that specific hash value. This property is related to the irreversibility of the hash function.

- **Collision Resistance**: It should be computationally infeasible to find two different inputs that produce the same hash value. Collisions weaken the security of hash functions, especially in cryptographic applications.

- **Efficient to Compute**: Hash functions need to be fast and efficient to compute, as they are widely used in various applications, including databases, digital signatures, and file integrity verification.

Bitcoin uses a specific hash function known as SHA-256 (Secure Hash Algorithm 256-bit). SHA-256 is a member of the SHA-2 family of cryptographic hash functions designed by the National Security Agency (NSA). It produces a 256-bit (32-byte) hash value and is widely used in various cryptographic applications due to its security properties. People say SHA-256 is safe from collision resistance, do you know why? The number of cases that could be represented with 256-bit is $2^{256}$. This number is bigger than the all atoms existing in the universe!!

## 3. Asymmetric key cryptography

Another major pillar for blockchain technology fundamentals is asymmetric key cryptography. Again intimidating terminology!

Before diving right into asymmetric key cryptography, it would be much easier to understand symmetric key cryptography first.

## Symmetric key cryptography

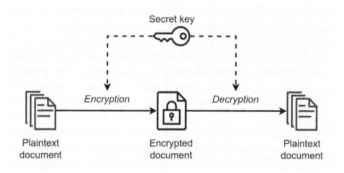

*Diagram of symmetric key cryptography. Source: Wikipedia*

Symmetric-key cryptography, also known as secret-key cryptography, is a cryptographic system that uses the same key for both the encryption of plaintext and the decryption of ciphertext. This means that the communicating parties must share a secret key before they can encrypt and decrypt messages. Symmetric-key algorithms are generally faster than their asymmetric counterparts, making them suitable for encrypting large amounts of data.

While reading this simple explanation, you are a crypto genius if you felt somewhat uncomfortable. If you look closely at the diagram, you could find out that the secret key is both used in encryption and decryption. Does it make a problem? The answer is "Absolutely YES!". Both parties who are encrypting and decrypting should have the same secret key, which leads to higher possibilities to be hacked.

## Asymmetric key cryptography

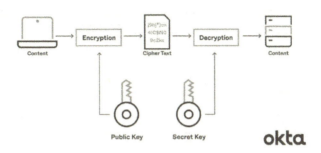

Diagram of Asymmetric key cryptography

Asymmetric key cryptography, also known as public-key cryptography, is a cryptographic system that uses a pair of keys for secure communication: a public key and a private key. These keys are mathematically related, but each key has a specific role in the encryption and decryption processes. The creation of keys are determined by an algorithm called ECDSA(Elliptic Curve Digital Signature Algorithm). If you first set up a private key, this algorithm will give you a public key. In bitcoin, your address is just a simple modification from this public key.

For a simple thought experiment, let's say there is a private key that can decrypt a message from a public key and vice-versa. Each key is the only key that can decrypt a message encrypted by the other key.

Now imagine Bob has declared a public key far and wide as the key that identifies him. Bob will keep a private key that corresponds to his public key. When he uses his private key to encrypt a message, he can share it publicly to be decrypted using his public key. Upon decrypting this message, we can say beyond the shadow of a doubt that only Bob could have written this message. The only key that could have encrypted the message is the corresponding private key which only Bob has access to. In practice, this would create an unforgeable digital signature for Bob.

On the flip side, what if a message was encrypted using Bob's public key? Of course, anyone can do this since Bob's public key is available to everyone. The benefit comes in that only Bob can decrypt the message. In this way, a friend of Bob's can write a message that can only be read by Bob. They could send it through any network, regardless of its security so long as it reaches Bob. They could rest assured that nobody would be able to decrypt the message except for Bob.

## 4. Merkle tree

There is one last concept you need to know before discussing Bitcoin. And that existence is a data structure called the "Merkle tree".

A Merkle tree, named after computer scientist Ralph Merkle, is a tree structure in which each leaf node represents a cryptographic hash of a data block, and each non-leaf node is a hash of its child nodes. The root of the tree, known as the Merkle root, is a single hash representing the entire set of data.

Let's understand this explanation by looking at this picture.

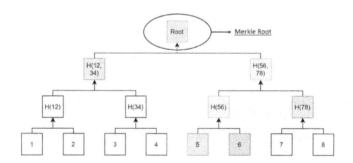

*Merkle Root is a total aggregated signature of all leaves in its tree, located at the very top. Source: simplilearn*

Earlier, we had just learned what a "hash function" is. Large "H" represents a hash function and numbers inside the parenthesis are the hashed arguments. For example H(12) means that it is an output of hashing number 1 and number 2 together. So in the above picture, number 1 from number

8(here we call them leaves) are hashed step by step and make the single Root which is called a Merkle root.

Just for a moment, I have a question for you! From only knowing the Merkle Root, is it possible to guess the leaf nodes? The answer is No! We have talked about some few key characteristics of a hash function and one of them was irreversibility. It is super easy to calculate the output from input. However, it's almost like finding a needle in a haystack to find input from a given output!

There is a very important functionality derived from this Merkle tree structure. And this groundbreaking functionality is called "Merkle Proof"

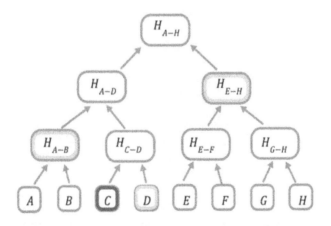

*Validating an element inside a Merkle tree needs log(N) elements, where N is the total number of the Merkle tree leaves. Source: Alchemy*

By given the Merkle tree($H_{A-H}$), if you want to validate number C whether it is in this Merkle tree, you only need 3 elements which are D, $H_{A-B}$ and $H_{E-H}$. This example shows how storing data inside a Merkle tree could be so powerful in terms of validating. If the total number of elements of the whole tree gets bigger and bigger, the required elements needed for proving decreases exponentially compared to its leaf number(In log scale). For example, we need 10 elements for a tree that has 1024 elements, we only need 10 elements more for a tree that has 1048576 elements.

# Bitcoin: A Peer-to-Peer Electronic Cash System

This is the holy grail paper in crypto space written in 2008 by an author under the pseudonym named Satoshi Nakamoto. I really recommend reading this paper if you came this far. It's only 9 pages long and you could probably understand at least half of the content since we have gone through the concepts of bit and byte, hash function, asymmetric key cryptography and Merkle tree!

## Bitcoin: A Peer-to-Peer Electronic Cash System

Satoshi Nakamoto
satoshin@gmx.com
www.bitcoin.org

**Abstract.** A purely peer-to-peer version of electronic cash would allow online payments to be sent directly from one party to another without going through a financial institution. Digital signatures provide part of the solution, but the main benefits are lost if a trusted third party is still required to prevent double-spending. We propose a solution to the double-spending problem using a peer-to-peer network. The network timestamps transactions by hashing them into an ongoing chain of hash-based proof-of-work, forming a record that cannot be changed without redoing the proof-of-work. The longest chain not only serves as proof of the sequence of events witnessed, but proof that it came from the largest pool of CPU power. As long as a majority of CPU power is controlled by nodes that are not cooperating to attack the network, they'll generate the longest chain and outpace attackers. The network itself requires minimal structure. Messages are broadcast on a best effort basis, and nodes can leave and rejoin the network at will, accepting the longest proof-of-work chain as proof of what happened while they were gone.

*First published Bitcoin white paper in 2008. Just by reading the "Abstract" part, it's sufficient to get a glimpse of this legendary paper.*

Bitcoin was created as a response to the growing need for an autonomous, decentralized digital currency, free from the control of governments and financial institutions. This need was particularly felt in the context of the 2008 financial crisis, which exposed the vulnerabilities of the traditional financial system. Bitcoin's creation was heavily influenced by the ideals and technical innovations of the cypherpunks.

Bitcoin was designed as a peer-to-peer network that operates without central authority, using cryptographic techniques to secure transactions, control the creation of new units, and verify the transfer of assets. Bitcoin's underlying technology, blockchain, ensures transparency and immutability of transactions, aligning with the cypherpunk vision of a system where privacy and security are paramount.

## How does the Bitcoin system work?

When it comes to learning a big subject, it is crucial for you to understand the holistic picture first and go into the details. Let's look at the step-by-step details of how the Bitcoin system works.

1. **Transaction Initiation**: A Bitcoin transaction begins when a user decides to send bitcoin to another user. The sender uses their private key to sign a transaction that includes the transaction amount, the receiver's public address, and the sender's public address.

2. **Transaction Verification**: Before a transaction is added to the blockchain, it must be verified by network participants, known as nodes. These nodes check the transaction's validity, ensuring that the sender has enough bitcoin and the transaction is properly signed.

3. **Transaction Pool**: Once verified, the transaction goes into a pool of unconfirmed transactions. Miners select transactions from this pool to form a new block.

4. **Mining Process**: Miners compete to solve a complex cryptographic puzzle, which requires significant computational power. This process is known as proof of work (PoW). The first miner to solve the puzzle gets the right to add the new block of transactions to the blockchain.

5. **Block Creation**: The winning miner assembles a block containing a set of verified transactions, the solution to the puzzle, and a reference to the previous block in the chain (the block's hash).

6.  **Block Addition**: Once a block is completed, it is broadcasted to the network. Other nodes then verify the validity of the solved puzzle and the transactions within the block. If everything checks out, each node adds this block to their copy of the blockchain.

7.  **Chain Continuation**: Each new block is chained to the previous block using cryptographic hashes. This chaining of blocks ensures the integrity of the blockchain and makes it tamper-resistant. Altering a single block would require recalculating every subsequent block's hash, an impractical task due to the network's collective computational power.

8.  **Consensus Protocol**: The Bitcoin blockchain operates on a consensus protocol, where the longest valid chain is accepted as the true version of events. This consensus is crucial in preventing double-spending and maintaining the integrity of the blockchain.

9.  **Rewarding Miners**: Miners are rewarded for their efforts in two ways: through new bitcoins created with each block (a process known as block reward) and through transaction fees paid by users. This incentivizes miners to contribute their computational power to the network.

10. **Decentralized Nature**: The distributed ledger of Bitcoin is maintained by a network of nodes, each having an identical copy of the blockchain. This decentralization ensures no single point of control or failure, enhancing the security and robustness of the network.

## Transaction initiation(1), Transaction verification(2)

For novices who first encounter the Bitcoin payment system get really confused because of its inherent structure. We are very familiar with the ledger based system, which our financial system selected for recording the amount of money. However, Bitcoin uses a different system and it's crucial to understand something called UTXO.

UTXOs, or Unspent Transaction Outputs, are a key concept in Bitcoin and some other cryptocurrencies, differing significantly from the ledger-based account model used in systems like Ethereum which we will further talk about in Chapter 3. In the UTXO model, there are no balances per individual; instead, individual UTXOs represent the digital currency available for a user to spend. Each Bitcoin transaction consumes one or more UTXOs as inputs and generates new UTXOs as outputs, which then become inputs for future transactions.

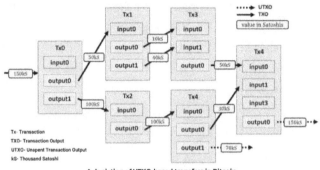

**A depiction of UTXO-based transfers in Bitcoin.**
Image by: Stefano Secci

*The Bitcoin system manages balance by UTXO. Unlike ledger based models, UTXO keeps track of who sent money to whom.*

When a user initiates a Bitcoin transaction, it involves inputs and outputs. Inputs refer to the funds being spent, and outputs represent the destination addresses where the funds are sent. There are two types of transaction, spent and unspent. After a transaction occurs, the output of that transaction is marked as spent. Unspent Transaction Outputs (UTXOs) are the remaining outputs that have not been used in subsequent transactions. Each UTXO represents a specific amount of bitcoin and is associated with a specific address.

For a better understanding, suppose you have 5 BTC in your wallet, and you decide to send 2 BTC to a friend. In this scenario, your wallet will create a transaction that consumes a UTXO of 5 BTC (the unspent output of a previous transaction to you) and creates two new UTXOs: one for your friend with 2 BTC and one for yourself with 3 BTC (the change). Keep in mind, the number of previous UTXOs and the number of subsequent UTXOs after the transaction do not need to be the same.

In contrast, the ledger-based account model, like that used in Ethereum, functions similarly to traditional bank accounts. Each account has a balance that is adjusted with each transaction. Transfers of value are direct and straightforward, continuously updating the account's state. The UTXO model provides enhanced privacy and flexibility since UTXOs are not directly tied to identities and can be fragmented. However, it can be less user-friendly due to the complexity of managing multiple UTXOs, and scalability can be an issue with the growth of the UTXO set. The account model, while simpler and more intuitive, potentially offers less privacy and poses challenges in parallelizing processing due to the interdependent nature of account balances.

## Transaction initiation happens in 3 steps

### 1. Creating the Transaction

- User Action: The process starts when a user (sender) decides to transfer bitcoins. Using a Bitcoin wallet, the sender initiates a transaction.
- Transaction Details: The transaction includes important details like the amount of bitcoin to send, the recipient's public address (where the bitcoin should go), and the sender's public address.

### 2. Digital Signature

- Securing the Transaction: The sender signs the transaction with their private key. This digital signature is crucial as it verifies the sender's ownership of the bitcoins and authorizes the transaction.
- Ensuring Integrity: The signature also safeguards the transaction from being altered by anyone else once it's been issued.

### 3. Broadcasting the Transaction

- Network Involvement: The signed transaction is broadcasted to the Bitcoin network. This is typically done via the sender's wallet software, which communicates with Bitcoin nodes (computers participating in the Bitcoin network).

## Transaction verification happens in 5 steps

### 1. Verification by Nodes

- Checking Authenticity: Nodes across the network receive the transaction and start the verification process. They check if the digital signature is valid using the sender's public key, confirming that the sender authorized the transaction.
- UTXO Checks: Nodes also verify that the inputs (the source of the bitcoins being sent) reference valid UTXOs (Unspent Transaction Outputs) and that they haven't been spent already.

### 2. Preventing Double-Spending

- Ensuring Single Use: Nodes check for double-spending to make sure the sender is not trying to spend the same bitcoins twice. This involves ensuring that each input in the transaction hasn't been used in a previous transaction that's already part of the blockchain.

### 3. Transaction Acceptance

- Mempool Entry: Once a transaction passes these verification checks, it gets accepted into the node's mempool (memory pool), a sort of holding area for transactions waiting to be included in a block.

### 4. Propagation to Other Nodes

- Spreading the Transaction: Using the gossip protocol, the transaction is relayed across the network. Each node that receives the transaction repeats the verification steps and, upon successful verification, passes it on to other nodes. A gossip protocol in computer science is a communication process used in distributed systems for nodes to exchange information efficiently and reliably by randomly selecting other nodes to share data with, akin to how rumors spread in social networks.

### 5. Awaiting Confirmation

- Inclusion in a Block: The transaction remains in the mempool until a miner selects it for inclusion in the next block. The time it takes to be included in a block depends on factors like network congestion and transaction fees offered by the sender.

The 'transaction initiation' phase in Bitcoin involves the creation, signing, and broadcasting of a transaction, while the 'transaction verification' phase involves nodes validating the transaction's authenticity, checking for double-spending, and then disseminating the transaction across the network. These steps ensure that all transactions are secure, legitimate, and ready to be added to the blockchain.

# Transaction pool(3)

In the Bitcoin blockchain, the 'transaction pool' or mempool plays a crucial role in managing the flow of transactions. It acts as a holding area for all verified but unconfirmed transactions, with each node in the network maintaining its own mempool. Transactions within the mempool are prioritized based on the fees attached to them, with those offering higher fees typically being selected first by miners for inclusion in new blocks. This prioritization becomes particularly significant during periods of high network congestion, where transactions with lower fees may face longer wait times for confirmation.

Miners select transactions from the mempool when assembling a new block, often opting for those with higher fees to maximize their earnings. Once a transaction is included in a mined block and the block is added to the blockchain, the transaction is considered confirmed and is subsequently removed from the mempool. The size of the mempool can vary, growing larger in times of increased network activity, and in such scenarios, nodes might drop transactions with the lowest fees to maintain efficiency.

The mempool thus serves as a dynamic space that balances the demand for transaction processing with the network's capacity to include transactions in the blockchain. It ensures that the Bitcoin network processes transactions efficiently while providing miners with the flexibility to prioritize transactions based on fee incentives, thereby maintaining the operational integrity and economic viability of the network.

## Mining process(4) + Consensus protocol(8), Rewarding Miners(9)

This phase is the core part of the blockchain system of blockchain. This is where something called consensus comes into play. You might have heard "Bitcoin miners are using tons of electricity for mining and earning tremendous profit" from the past news. All this mining is happening because bitcoin is designed with this consensus called PoW(Proof Of Work). Before going right into the consensus, let's have a brief look at how the Bitcoin block looks like.

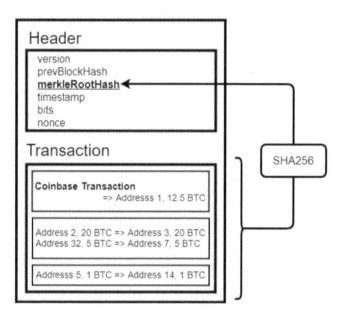

*Header is consisted of 6 different fields. Only the Merkle root of the transaction data is uploaded in the block header for storage efficiency.*

In a Bitcoin block, the block header and the transaction part are integral components. The block header is a compact summary that includes crucial elements like the version, the hash of the previous block (linking the blocks in the blockchain), the Merkle Root (a hash of all transactions ensuring their integrity), the timestamp (recording when the block was created), the difficulty target (indicating the mining difficulty), and the nonce (used in the mining process). This header plays a vital role in maintaining the blockchain's continuity and security.

The transaction part of the block contains all the transactions processed in that block. It lists the number of transactions and details of each transaction, including sender and receiver addresses, transaction amounts, and unique identifiers. Each transaction comprises inputs and outputs, detailing the flow of bitcoins. Together, the block header and the transaction part ensure the efficient functioning and robust security of the Bitcoin network, recording transactions and maintaining the blockchain's immutable structure.

## What is consensus? What is PoW?

The word "Consensus" in Bitcoin means an agreement made between nodes that which block should be added in the canonical chain, which chain should be the legit one(We will talk about the fork right below). In Bitcoin, it follows a consensus named Nakamoto Consensus.

Nakamoto Consensus is a term used to describe the specific consensus mechanism employed by Bitcoin, as introduced by its creator, Satoshi Nakamoto. It is a novel approach that combines several components to achieve consensus on the state of the blockchain in a decentralized and trustless environment. Nakamoto Consensus is constituted in two parts, PoW(Proof Of Work) and the longest chain rule.

## PoW (Proof of Work)

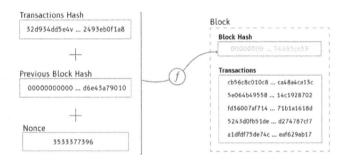

*The hash of a block is the combination of several elements including: transactions hash, previous block hash, nonce plus index, timestamp and data. Miner's work is to find a nonce that makes the hash value of the block to be below a certain range. "f" in the above image refers to a hashing function.*
*Source: paymentandbanking*

Proof of Work (PoW) in Bitcoin is a consensus mechanism where miners compete to solve a cryptographic puzzle by repeatedly changing a 32-bit field called the nonce in the block header to generate new hashes, aiming to find one that makes the Hash(Index + previous hash + timestamp + data + nonce) to be less than a certain number(Check the previous image that depicts what comprises the Bitcoin block). The first miner to solve the puzzle gets the right to add a new block of transactions to the blockchain. This process is crucial for securing the network and validating transactions, repeats millions and billions of times until a valid hash is discovered.

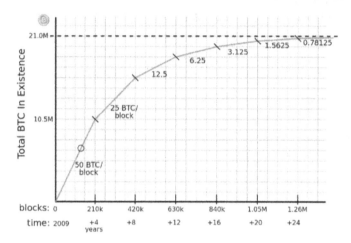

*Bitcoin halving occurs every 4 years, starting from 2008. Source: Yaşar Gültekin*

Miners who successfully solve the puzzle not only gets the right for adding a block to the blockchain but also rewarded with newly created bitcoins, known as the block reward, which is halved approximately every four years in an event called "halving," initially set at 50 bitcoins per block and gradually decreasing to control inflation. This is almost $2.1M dollars in today's value. It's insane that if you had mined bitcoin in 2008, you might have earned $2.1M dollars for every 10 minutes! Miners also collect transaction fees from users, providing an additional incentive especially as the block reward diminishes over time, thereby ensuring the ongoing health and security of the network.

Did you know there is a strong correlation between Bitcoin price and its halving period? Historically, Bitcoin halving events have been associated with significant increases in Bitcoin's price, as they reinforce Bitcoin's perception as a scarce asset, potentially boosting its appeal as a store of value.

The impact of Bitcoin halving on its price can be understood through the lens of supply and demand economics. If the demand for Bitcoin remains constant or increases while the rate of new supply growth slows down, the price should theoretically rise. This principle, coupled with market anticipation and speculative behavior, often leads to increased buying activity before and after a halving. However, it's important to note that the cryptocurrency market is influenced by a multitude of factors, and the direct impact of halving on Bitcoin's price can vary.

*ASIC is a specified device for computing Bitcoin puzzles(left).*
*Mining farm holding thousands of ASIC(right).*

Nowadays there are special devices designed to find the nonce values in Bitcoin. This device is called ASIC(Application-Specific Integrated Circuit) which are custom-built chips created to perform the calculations required for mining with much greater efficiency than general-purpose hardware like CPUs or GPUs. Some companies own a bitcoin mining farm like in the right picture so it became almost impossible to mine the block reward on an individual level.

The mechanism behind proof-of-work was a breakthrough in crypto space because it simultaneously solved two problems. First, it provided a simple and moderately effective consensus algorithm, allowing nodes in the network to collectively agree on a set of canonical updates to the state of the Bitcoin ledger. Second, it provided a mechanism for allowing free entry into the consensus process, solving the political problem of deciding who gets to influence the consensus, while simultaneously preventing sybil attacks. It does this by substituting a formal barrier to participation, such as the requirement to be registered as a unique entity on a particular list, with an economic barrier - the weight of a single node in the consensus voting process is directly proportional to the computing power that the node brings.

Since then, an alternative approach has been proposed called *proof-of-stake*(we will talk about this in Chapter 3 Ethereum part!), calculating the weight of a node as being proportional to its currency holdings and not computational resources. Lots of layer1 blockchains are switching into PoS from PoW for better energy consumption and scalability.

## Longest chain rule

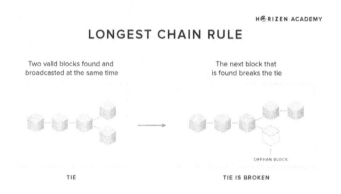

*Longest chain rule decides which chain to be a canonical chain when the chain is forked by considering the length.*

The longest chain rule dictates that the valid version of the blockchain is the one with the longest sequence of blocks, or more accurately, the chain that has accumulated the most computational work. This rule becomes crucial in instances of temporary forks(explained right below section), where two valid blocks are produced simultaneously, leading to two versions of the blockchain. In such cases, the blockchain that becomes longer first, as more blocks are added, is recognized as the valid one.

This rule plays a vital role in maintaining consensus across the decentralized network of nodes, ensuring that all participants agree on a single version of the blockchain without the need for a central authority. It also fortifies the network against certain types of attacks, such as the alteration of confirmed transactions, which would require re-mining not only the targeted block but also all subsequent blocks to create a longer chain—a task that is computationally impractical in large networks. Additionally, the longest chain rule incentivizes miners to work on the longest chain, as blocks mined on shorter forks, known as orphaned blocks, do not yield rewards. This incentivization is key to encouraging miners to contribute to the network's security and integrity.

## What is a fork?

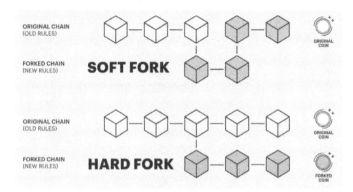

*To put it simply, soft fork is like updating a software where hard fork is migrating to completely new software. If a hard fork happens, the forked chain needs a new native coin since the chain is not compatible with the previous chain anymore.*
*Source: tangem*

"Fork" refers to a divergence in the blockchain that occurs when there are two or more potential paths forward. This can happen in any blockchain-based system. Forks are categorized mainly into two types: soft forks and hard forks. Let's see the difference by a table.

| Feature | Hard Fork | Soft Fork |
|---|---|---|
| Backward Compatibility | Not backward-compatible. | Backward-compatible. |
| Creation of New Currency | Can lead to the creation of a new cryptocurrency (e.g., Bitcoin Cash). | Does not lead to the creation of a new currency. |
| Community Agreement | Often occurs due to a lack of consensus within the community. | Requires a high level of consensus within the community. |
| Result | Results in a permanent divergence in the blockchain, creating two separate chains. | Introduces new rules that are backward-compatible, maintaining a single chain. |

*Differences between Hard Fork vs Soft Fork*

These are the cryptocurrencies that are hard forked from the original Bitcoin. I guess you might understand now why there are so many different cryptocurrencies that have a prefix with Bitcoin!

| Cryptocurrency | Hard Fork Date | Reason |
|---|---|---|
| Bitcoin Cash (BCH) | August 1, 2017 | Disagreement over the block size limit; increased block size to 8 MB. |
| Bitcoin Gold (BTG) | October 24, 2017 | Aimed to decentralize mining by changing the proof-of-work algorithm. |
| Bitcoin Diamond (BCD) | November 24, 2017 | Increased block size and changed mining algorithm for improved privacy and lower fees. |
| Bitcoin Private (BTCP) | February 28, 2018 | Combined privacy features of Zclassic with the Bitcoin blockchain. |
| Bitcoin SV (BSV) | November 15, 2018 | Contentious hard fork within the Bitcoin Cash community. |
| Bitcoin Cash ABC (BCHA) | November 15, 2018 | Implemented changes in the Bitcoin Cash protocol, introducing new features. |

*Whole a lot of hard forks happened to Bitcoin!*

## Block creation(5), Block addition(6), Chain continuation(7)

The "block creation" phase involves miners selecting transactions from the mempool and engaging in the mining process, which requires Proof of Work (PoW). This phase includes constructing a block header that references the previous block, thereby linking the new block to the existing chain. Once the puzzle is solved, the miner assembles the block by combining the header with the chosen transactions.

The "block addition" phase starts when the newly created block is broadcasted to the network. Other nodes then independently verify its validity, including the correctness of the PoW and the legitimacy of the transactions. Upon successful verification, the block is added to the blockchain, updating the ledger across all nodes. The miner who created the block is rewarded with newly minted bitcoins and transaction fees from the transactions included in the block.

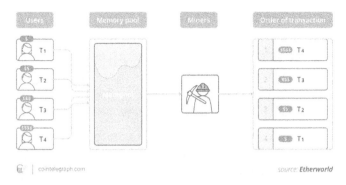

*The fastest miner wins the block award and also determines the order of transactions for that block!*

Miners select transactions from the mempool, a collection of unconfirmed transactions, to include in a new block. The primary criterion for selection is the transaction fee; those offering higher fees are typically given priority, as miners aim to maximize their profits. Additionally, the size of transactions plays a role, with miners balancing the transaction size against the fees they offer. Miners must also adhere to specific network rules and protocols, which dictate transaction eligibility for block inclusion.

Miners also consider transaction dependencies, ensuring that transactions dependent on others are confirmed in the correct order. Different miners might employ various strategies for selecting transactions, influenced by personal policies or goals. Lastly, the block size limit is a crucial factor, as miners ensure the total size of the selected transactions does not exceed this limit. This process determines which transactions are confirmed once the miner successfully adds a new block to the blockchain.

Finally, the "chain continuation" phase ensures the blockchain's ongoing growth and security. After a block is added, miners immediately begin working on the next block, thus continuously extending the blockchain. This process not only secures the network by making it increasingly difficult to alter past transactions but also adapts to the network's total computational power through periodic adjustments of the PoW difficulty. This cycle is critical for maintaining the functionality, security, and integrity of the Bitcoin network.

## The decentralized nature(10)

Bitcoin's decentralized nature stems from its design as a distributed ledger (blockchain) managed by a network of nodes worldwide, with no central authority. Transactions are recorded on this public ledger, secured through a consensus mechanism known as Proof of Work, where miners use computational power to validate transactions and add them to the blockchain. This process, coupled with the peer-to-peer network structure, ensures that control and decision-making are spread across a diverse set of participants.

Key to Bitcoin's decentralization is its open-source software, allowing for transparent and communal decision-making regarding protocol changes. The cryptographic security inherent in Bitcoin protects the integrity of transactions and user autonomy, while the built-in incentive system ensures a distributed group of miners maintain the network. This decentralized architecture makes Bitcoin resistant to censorship and central control, offering users full control over their transactions without reliance on traditional centralized financial institutions.

# Chapter 3

# Ethereum, unlocking a world of smart contracts and dApps

## Birth of Ethereum

*"Turing machine", a general computing system with predefined rules, was named after the father of computer Alan Turing(left). There is a famous rumor that apple's logo is said to have been taken from the bitten apple when Alan Turing ended his life by suicide(right).*

Have you heard of a guy named Alan Turing? Alan Turing(left picture) was a British computer scientist, mathematician, and cryptanalyst, was a pioneering figure in the field of computer science and artificial intelligence. He is best known for his work during World War II at Bletchley Park, where he played a crucial role in breaking the German Enigma code, a significant contribution to the Allied war effort. Turing is also considered the father of theoretical computer science and artificial intelligence, and he developed the concept of the Turing machine.

Unfortunately, he faced legal and social persecution for his homosexuality and tragically died from cyanide poisoning in 1954, which was ruled a suicide. A partly eaten apple was found beside his bed, leading to speculation that he had ingested the cyanide through the apple.

One of his monumental efforts was creating a concept called 'Turing complete'. "Turing complete" describes a system or programming language's ability to simulate a Turing machine, a theoretical model of computation. If a system is Turing complete, it can solve any computationally solvable problem given sufficient time and resources. Key features include universal computation, conditional branching, looping, and memory storage. Popular programming languages like Python, Java, and C++ are considered Turing complete. Being Turing complete doesn't address efficiency or practicality for specific tasks; it signifies the theoretical computational power and versatility of a system.

Ethereum was created to address key limitations in Bitcoin's blockchain technology, primarily its lack of Turing completeness, value-blindness, absence of state, and blockchain-blindness. Unlike Bitcoin's scripting language, which is intentionally limited to avoid issues like infinite loops, Ethereum introduced a Turing-complete language, allowing for more complex and versatile computations. This advancement enabled the development of sophisticated contracts and decentralized applications. Ethereum's design overcomes the restrictions of Bitcoin's UTXO model, enabling fine-grained transaction control and the ability to retain internal states within contracts. This capability is vital for creating multi-stage financial agreements and decentralized autonomous organizations. Additionally, Ethereum's awareness of blockchain-specific data, like nonce and timestamps, opens new possibilities for applications needing elements of randomness or blockchain data reliance. By surmounting these limitations, Ethereum established itself as a more adaptable and powerful platform for a wide array of blockchain applications.

*Vitalik Buterin(left) and Dr.Gavin Wood(right). Both became
a historical figure in crypto space by creating Ethereum,
opening a new era with smart contracts and dApps.*

Ethereum's inception can be largely attributed to Vitalik Buterin, a visionary programmer deeply involved in the cryptocurrency community. Disillusioned by Bitcoin's limitations, particularly its simplistic scripting language, Buterin wrote the Ethereum white paper in 2013. This seminal document proposed a blockchain platform that extended beyond Bitcoin's financial applications, introducing the idea of immutable, programmable contracts and applications through a unique scripting language. Buterin's concept aimed to leverage blockchain technology for a broader range of applications, far surpassing Bitcoin's capabilities.

ETHEREUM: A SECURE DECENTRALISED GENERALISED TRANSACTION LEDGER
LONDON VERSION 818564b — 2023-11-30

DR. GAVIN WOOD
FOUNDER, ETHEREUM & PARITY
GAVIN@PARITY.IO

ABSTRACT. The blockchain paradigm when coupled with cryptographically-secured transactions has demonstrated its utility through a number of projects, with Bitcoin being one of the most notable ones. Each such project can be seen as a simple application on a decentralised, but singleton, compute resource. We can call this paradigm a transactional singleton machine with shared-state.

Ethereum implements this paradigm in a generalised manner. Furthermore it provides a plurality of such resources, each with a distinct state and operating code but able to interact through a message-passing framework with others. We discuss its design, implementation issues, the opportunities it provides and the future hurdles we envisage.

*Ethereum yellow paper, including technical details of EVM and
Ethereum protocol specifications, written by Dr.Gavin Wood.*

Gavin Wood, a British computer programmer, was instrumental in Ethereum's early development. He authored the Ethereum Yellow Paper, which detailed the Ethereum Virtual Machine (EVM) - a key innovation for running smart contracts. The EVM, as conceived by Wood, made Ethereum Turing-complete, allowing it to execute complex contracts and host decentralized applications. This Turing-completeness, enabled

Ethereum to perform any computation, given sufficient time and resources, significantly broadening its potential uses beyond those of Bitcoin.

Let's see what Ethereum could solve, which Bitcoin could not in much more detail.

**Lack of Turing-completeness** - The problem about turing completeness was an inherently crucial problem of Bitcoin so we are going to point out one more time with detail. While there is a large subset of computation that the Bitcoin scripting language supports, it does not nearly support everything. The main category that is missing is loops(i.e. "for" loops in computer science). This is done to avoid infinite loops during transaction verification; theoretically it is a surmountable obstacle for script programmers, since any loop can be simulated by simply repeating the underlying code many times with an if statement, but it does lead to scripts that are very space-inefficient. For example, implementing an alternative elliptic curve signature algorithm would likely require 256 repeated multiplication rounds all individually included in the code.

**Value-blindness** - "Value blindness" in the Bitcoin system refers to a limitation in its transaction scripting mechanism, particularly with the Unspent Transaction Output (UTXO) model. In Bitcoin, a UTXO can either be spent in its entirety or not at all; there is no native mechanism for a script to partially spend or control the amount that is being transacted. This is fundamentally different from traditional bank accounts where you can spend any portion of your balance.

This limitation becomes apparent in complex financial contracts or applications where nuanced control over transaction amounts is necessary. For instance, in a scenario where two parties enter into a contract that dictates specific amounts to be paid based on certain conditions, Bitcoin's value-blind nature makes this difficult to implement directly. Each UTXO has a fixed value and the script cannot dictate that only a portion of it be spent under certain conditions.

**Lack of state** - UTXO can either be spent or unspent; there is no opportunity for multi-stage contracts or scripts which keep any other internal state beyond that(on the other hand, ethereum is basically a state machine). This makes it hard to make multi-stage options contracts, decentralized exchange offers or two-stage cryptographic commitment protocols (necessary for secure computational bounties). It also means that UTXO can only be used to build simple, one-off contracts and not more complex "stateful" contracts such as decentralized organizations, and makes meta-protocols difficult to implement. Binary state combined with value-blindness also mean that another important application, withdrawal limits, is impossible.

**Blockchain-blindness** - UTXO is blind to blockchain data such as the nonce, the timestamp and previous block hash. This severely limits applications in gambling, and several other categories, by depriving the scripting language of a potentially valuable source of randomness.

## Introducing the EVM

EVM is a runtime environment for executing smart contracts on the Ethereum network. It provides a decentralized, Turing-complete virtual machine that allows developers to write smart contracts using various programming languages. A smart contract is a self-executing contract with the terms of the agreement directly written into lines of code, which automatically enforces and executes the terms when predetermined conditions are met.

We have had a peek on what is turing-complete in the start of this chapter. By the way, what is a smart contract and what is a runtime environment?

Smart contract is a self-executing agreement with terms written in code, running on a blockchain, like Ethereum. It automatically enforces and executes the terms of a contract when predetermined conditions are met, without the need for intermediaries. Smart contracts are immutable once deployed, which means they cannot be changed, and they are distributed, meaning the output of the contract is validated by everyone on the network. This technology enables trustless and transparent transactions, making them ideal for a wide range of applications like financial services, supply chain management, and automated governance systems. Their self-executing nature reduces the risk of fraud and lowers the costs associated with traditional contracts, offering a more efficient, secure, and automated approach to contract enforcement

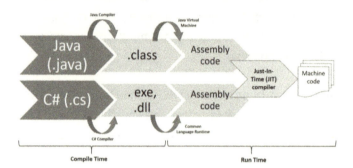

*Sequential flow of how high level languages are converted into machine code. Run time happens after a compile time.*

A runtime environment in computer science is a crucial component for executing a program, providing necessary services like memory management and interfacing with the system's hardware and operating system. It acts during the execution phase of a program, different from the compile-time phase. Compile-time refers to the period when source code is translated into executable code by a compiler. This process includes syntax analysis, optimization, and code generation, preparing the program for execution.

The runtime environment then takes over, offering a platform-independent framework that allows the compiled code to run consistently across various systems. This integration of compile-time and runtime processes ensures that a program is correctly translated and efficiently executed, regardless of the underlying hardware or operating system. By providing a standardized environment, these systems ensure consistent behavior of applications regardless of where and how they are executed.

So putting this all together, EVM is simply a globally decentralized machine that operates as a runtime environment of smart contracts which were originally written by a human in a higher language like solidity(we will learn about this language at the end of this chapter).

## Ethereum world state

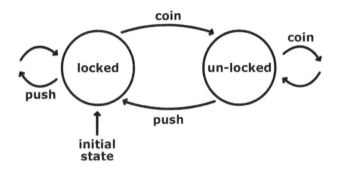

*A simple state machine as an example. Here, the state is changed as locked/un-locked by inserting coin or pushing a door.*

State is like a current image of the functioning system. For a better understanding, let's again have a thought experiment. Imagine there is a turnstile machine that turns into an unlock state when a coin is inserted. And there is two possible state which are "locked" and "un-locked" for this system to have. As for an initial state, turnstile is locked. There is again two possible acts you could do in this state, whether push the turnstile or inserting a coin. It would stay locked forever when you just push the turnstile. However, if you insert a coin, it turns into a "un-locked" state. And a similar procedure occurs when the state is in "un-locked" state as well.

The Ethereum Virtual Machine (EVM) can be understood as a state machine, where its state represents the collective state of all accounts and smart contracts, including their balances, storage, and code. Every transaction in Ethereum transitions the EVM from one state to another, following a set of rules defined by the Ethereum protocol, with transactions being the inputs that trigger state transitions.

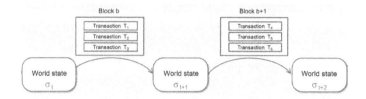

*Ethereum world state is a singleton pattern which means it exists only as a single instance. It's state changes by the occurring transactions.*

In the broad picture, this flow shows pretty much everything of how the EVM works. There is a world state that is changed by the transaction that happened on the time-frame. There were only two states in the turnstile case, however in EVM the state is changed by every block creation time and does not go backwards.

World state $\sigma_t$

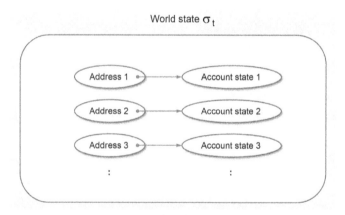

*Ethereum world state is simply recording multiple account's state with it's corresponding address.*

What state in Ethereum is actually doing is just keeping records of how the state of account is changed over time. Inside the state there is a key-value mapping of the account address and its account state. Simple, huh?

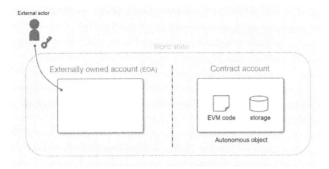

*There are two types of Ethereum account, Externally owned account(EOA) and Contract account(CA).*

There are two different types of accounts in EVM. One is EOA(Externally Owned Account) and the other one is CA(Contract Account). EOAs are accounts controlled by private keys. These are the accounts that individuals use to hold and transfer Ether (ETH) and interact with the Ethereum network. Plus, EOAs are typically associated with human users and are used for personal transactions and holding funds.

Contract accounts are accounts that are associated with smart contracts. Unlike EOAs, they don't have a private key associated with them. Instead, their behavior is governed by the code of the smart contract. In CA's code execution, transactions sent to contract accounts trigger the execution of the contract's code, potentially modifying the contract's state or triggering other actions.

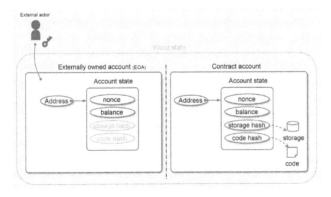

*Contract account keeps additional information which are storage hash and code hash.*

There are some differences between EOA and CA about what kinds of fields are stored inside. Let's dissect one by one.

### Nonce

- The nonce is a counter associated with each account.
- For EOA, the nonce represents the number of transactions sent from that account. It helps prevent replay attacks(an attack where a malicious actor uses a verified signature more than twice which were proposed to be used only once).
- For CA, the nonce is the number of contract-creating transactions sent from the controlling EOA. It ensures the order and integrity of contract executions.

### Balance

- The balance is the amount of Ether (ETH) associated with the account.
- For EOAs, the balance represents the amount of Ether that the account can transfer.
- For CAs, the balance represents the amount of Ether the contract holds. Contracts can receive and send Ether based on their logic.

### Code Hash

- The code hash represents the hash of the contract's bytecode.
- For EOAs, the code hash is not applicable, as they don't have associated code.
- For CAs, the code hash is used to verify the integrity of the contract's code. It allows clients to quickly check whether a contract's code has changed.

### Storage

- Storage represents the key-value storage associated with contract accounts.

- Contracts can store persistent data in their storage, and each contract has its own storage space.
- Storage is organized in a key-value structure and is used to maintain the state of a contract between transactions.

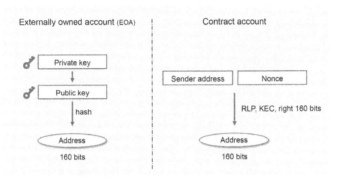

*The mechanism of how an address is created is different between EOA and CA.*

How is the address value determined? The determination of an address in EOA is similar to how a Bitcoin address is made. First you choose a private key and public key derived using ECDSA(Elliptic Curve Digital Signature Algorithm). The final EOA address is just truncating a few digits from the beginning of the public key and making it into 160 bits.

In CA, an address is created from the sender's address and a nonce. Nonce is a special counter that increases by one whenever a new account is created from the sender. This is to prevent creating the same address. There is also a new method to make an address with an CREATE2 opcode. This does not need nonce, instead this requires some random number called salt, sender's address and the bytecode of the contract.

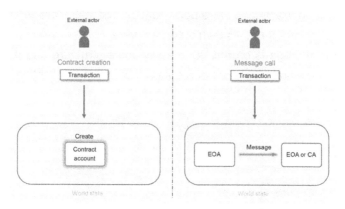

*External actor can send two types of transactions. One is creating a new CA. The other one is sending a message to existing EOA or CA.*

Something that you should keep in mind is that only EOA can initiate a transaction. There are two kinds of transactions which EOA could initiate. One is creating a brand new CA and the other one is giving a message call to existing EOA or CA.

In Ethereum, a message call involves sending a message from one account to another, either between EOAs or from an EOA to a CA. Message calls are essential for transferring Ether (ETH) between users and interacting with smart contracts. Gas is required for every message call to cover computational costs, and users pay gas fees. When an EOA interacts with a smart contract, the contract's code is executed, and its state may be modified. Message calls can include return values and events, allowing users to retrieve information and log specific actions on the blockchain. Overall, message calls facilitate communication and value transfer within the decentralized Ethereum network.

## Gas

In Ethereum, "gas" is a measurement unit for the computational effort required to execute transactions and smart contracts on the network. Each operation requires a certain amount of gas, with more complex operations consuming more. The cost of gas is determined by the gas price, which is the amount of Ether (ETH) the user is willing to pay per gas unit, typically quoted in "gwei," a smaller denomination of ETH.

Gas serves as a protective mechanism to prevent network abuse, limiting the amount of computational work a transaction or operation can consume. The Ethereum network also imposes a block gas limit, which caps the total gas used by all transactions in a block. This limit is crucial for maintaining network performance and avoiding excessive block sizes.

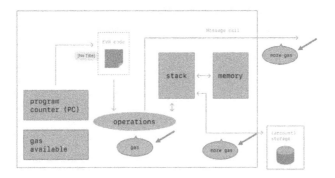

*If allocated gas gets depleted in the middle of executing a transaction, the entire transaction gets reverted and the rest of the unused gas gets refunded.*

Upon creation, each transaction is charged with a certain amount of gas that has to be paid for by the originator of the transaction (tx.origin). While the EVM executes the transaction, the gas is gradually depleted according to specific rules. If the gas is used up at any point (i.e. it would be negative), an out-of-gas exception is triggered, which ends execution and reverts all modifications made to the state in the current call frame.

This mechanism incentivizes economical use of EVM execution time and also compensates EVM executors (i.e. miners / stakers) for their work. Since each block has a maximum amount of gas, it also limits the amount of work needed to validate a block. Higher gas prices can lead to faster transaction processing as they are more appealing to miners.

The gas price is a value set by the originator of the transaction, who has to pay gas_price * gas up front to the EVM executor. If some gas is left after execution, it is refunded to the transaction originator. In case of an exception that reverts changes, already used up gas is not refunded.

## Storage, Memory and Stack

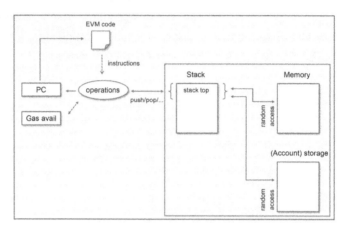

*Stack, Memory and (Account) storage are the places where information is stored in EVM.*

The Ethereum Virtual Machine has three areas where it can store data: storage, memory and the stack.

Each account has a data area called storage, which is persistent between function calls and transactions. Storage is a key-value store that maps 256-bit words to 256-bit words. It is not possible to enumerate storage from within a contract, it is comparatively costly to read, and even more expensive to initialize and modify storage. Because of this cost, you should minimize what you store in persistent storage to what the contract needs to run. Store data like derived calculations, caching, and aggregates outside of the contract. A contract can neither read nor write to any storage apart from its own.

The second data area is called memory, of which a contract obtains a freshly cleared instance for each message call. Memory is linear and can be addressed at byte level, but reads are limited to a width of 256 bits, while writes can be either 8 bits or 256 bits wide. Memory is expanded by a word (256-bit), when accessing (either reading or writing) a previously untouched memory word (i.e. any offset within a word). At the time of expansion, the cost in gas must be paid. Memory is more costly the larger it grows (it scales quadratically).

The EVM is not a register machine but a stack machine, so all computations are performed on a data area called the stack. The third data area called stack has a maximum size of 1024 elements and contains words of 256 bits. Access to the stack is limited to the top end in the following way: It is possible to copy one of the topmost 16 elements to the top of the stack or swap the topmost element with one of the 16 elements below it. All other operations take the topmost two (or one, or more, depending on the operation) elements from the stack and push the result onto the stack. Of course it is possible to move stack elements to storage or memory in order to get deeper access to the stack, but it is not possible to just access arbitrary elements deeper in the stack without first removing the top of the stack.

# Proof of Stake and Ethereum 2.0

Proof of Stake (PoS) is a consensus mechanism used in blockchain networks to achieve agreement on the state of the blockchain and validate transactions. Unlike Proof of Work (PoW), where participants (miners) compete to solve complex puzzles, PoS relies on validators who are chosen to create new blocks based on the amount of cryptocurrency they hold and are willing to "stake" as collateral.

These are the key characteristics of PoS consensus.

### Selection and Role of Validators in PoS Systems

- In Proof of Stake (PoS) systems, validators, who are responsible for creating new blocks and validating transactions, are selected based on their willingness to lock up a certain amount of cryptocurrency as collateral, known as a "stake." This staking process serves as an economic incentive for validators to maintain honest behavior, as their stake is at risk. The selection of validators can vary, with some PoS algorithms choosing randomly, while others may consider factors like the amount staked and the age of the coins.

## Process of Block Creation and Validation

- Selected validators undertake the task of creating new blocks containing transactions, which are then added to the blockchain. These blocks are subsequently validated by other validators to ensure the legitimacy of the transactions and the honesty of the block creator. If the block is accepted by the network, validators are rewarded, typically with transaction fees and sometimes newly minted cryptocurrency. This reward system motivates validators to participate honestly in the consensus process.

## Network Security, Penalties, and Environmental Impact

- PoS systems incorporate mechanisms for penalizing validators who act maliciously or try to manipulate the network, often involving the forfeiture of their staked cryptocurrency. Additionally, to prevent centralization and ensure network decentralization, PoS often includes a system for periodically rotating validators. The security of PoS lies in its ability to achieve finality, ensuring that once a block is added, it's improbable to be reversed. Notably, PoS is lauded for its energy efficiency compared to Proof of Work (PoW) systems, reducing the environmental impact commonly associated with cryptocurrency mining.

| Feature | Proof of Work (PoW) | Proof of Stake (PoS) |
|---|---|---|
| Validation Process | Miners solve complex puzzles to propose new blocks. | Validators chosen based on stake or other factors. |
| Resource Consumption | Requires significant computational power and energy. | More energy-efficient, relies on participants staking coins. |
| Security Model | Achieves security through computational work. | Relies on economic incentives and collateral. |
| Decentralization | Generally considered decentralized, but mining power can concentrate. | Aims for decentralization, but concerns about wealth concentration. |
| Example | Bitcoin uses PoW. | Ethereum 2.0 is transitioning to PoS. |

*PoW vs PoS. These days, most of the layer1 blockchain uses PoS as their consensus mechanism due to superior energy efficiency and scalability.*

*Ethereum finally turned it's consensus mechanism from PoW to PoS.*

The transition from PoW to PoS in Ethereum, known as "The Merge," was a major milestone in the network's development. The process involved several key steps and stages:

- **Development and Testing**: Prior to The Merge, Ethereum developers created and extensively tested the new PoS blockchain, known as the Beacon Chain, which ran parallel to the existing PoW chain.

- **Beacon Chain Launch**: The Beacon Chain was launched in December 2020. This did not immediately change the main Ethereum chain; it was a separate PoS network meant to test and prepare for the eventual switchover.

- **Validator Participation**: Users could participate as validators in the Beacon Chain by staking their Ethereum tokens (ETH). This required locking a minimum of 32 ETH into a deposit contract.

- **The Merge**: The actual transition, called "The Merge," involved merging the original Ethereum PoW chain with the new Beacon Chain. This was a highly coordinated upgrade where the PoW mechanism was turned off, and the PoS consensus mechanism took over.

- **Post-Merge Upgrades**: Following The Merge, further upgrades were planned to improve and optimize the network. These include the Shanghai/Capella upgrade and others focused on scalability and additional functionalities.

## Merkle Patricia Trie

We have learned what "Merkle tree" is in the previous Chapter. Ethereum uses data structure that is one step further than Merkle tree which is called "Merkle Patrica Trie".

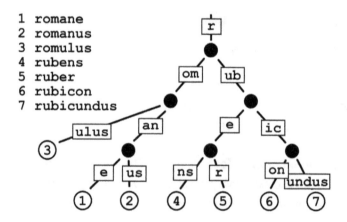

*A Patricia trie, also called as Radix trie, is a tree-like data structure that is used to retrieve a string value by traversing down a branch of nodes that store associated references(keys) that together lead to the end value that can be returned. Source: Alchemy*

The Merkle Patricia Trie is a complex data structure that merges the concepts of a Merkle tree and a Patricia trie (Radix trie). This combination results in a highly efficient and secure method of storing and looking up all (key, value) bindings data. In the context of Ethereum, it's primarily used for storing the state, which includes account balances, contract code, and storage.

It is also fully deterministic, meaning that tries with the same (key, value) bindings are guaranteed to be identical - down to the last byte. This means that they have the same root hash, providing the holy grail of O(log(n)) efficiency for inserts, lookups and deletes. Moreover, they are simpler to understand and code than more complex comparison-based alternatives, like red-black trees.

## Merkle Patricia Tries in Ethereum

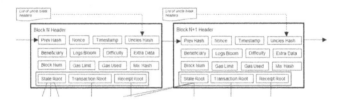

*Inside the Ethereum block there are three roots which are State root, Transaction root and Receipt root. Source: Alchemy*

These three Merkle Patricia roots in a block's header serve as anchors of trust and verification. They enable nodes in the network to quickly and efficiently verify the integrity and consistency of the blockchain's state, transactions, and their outcomes, ensuring the blockchain's security and reliability.

The state root is a cryptographic hash that represents the entire state of the Ethereum blockchain at a particular point in time. This includes balances, contract code, and all account information. It's a part of the block's header and is generated using Merkle Patricia Tree data structure. Each time a transaction occurs, it alters the state of the network, resulting in a new state root. This continuous updating ensures that the state root reflects the most current state of all data on the Ethereum blockchain.

The transaction root, also known as the "transactions trie root," is another cryptographic hash included in the block's header. It represents all the transactions included in that specific block. Each transaction in the block is hashed, and these hashes are used to create a Merkle Tree. The root of this tree is the transaction root. This mechanism ensures that all transactions in the block are accounted for and have not been tampered with.

The receipt root, sometimes referred to as the "receipts trie root," is a hash of all receipts from the transactions in a block. A receipt is generated for each transaction and includes information such as the transaction's status (success or failure), the gas used, and any logs that were generated. These receipts are hashed and organized into a Merkle Tree, with the root of this tree being the receipt root. This provides a verifiable way to quickly check the outcome and effect of each transaction in a block without re-executing them.

## Solidity

In this section, I know it would be hard for readers who do not have any programming background might have a hard time going through this part. However, I have included this part since, it gives you a better understanding if you know how the smart contract is written under the hood. It's fine if you could just skip this whole part. Just think of it as a supplementary reading. My only intention here is to give you a glimpse of how the smart contract is actually written. Here, we are going to learn the basic syntax of solidity and some simple smart contracts that act as a simple storage and minting a new coin!

Solidity, as a programming language designed for blockchain development, particularly Ethereum, stands distinct from traditional programming languages in several key aspects. One of the primary differences is its operation within a global state stored on the blockchain, where deployed code is immutable, unlike traditional languages where code can be modified and variables often have local scope. Solidity's focus on blockchain-centric design sets it apart from general-purpose languages, which are not inherently tied to decentralized systems.

Developers using Solidity must also be acutely aware of gas costs, as executing code on the blockchain incurs fees, necessitating code optimization to manage these costs — a consideration typically absent in traditional programming environments.

In Solidity, smart contracts are treated as first-class citizens, with the language offering specific constructs for their development. This contrasts with traditional languages, where concepts like smart contracts or a shared global state in a decentralized network are absent.

Additionally, Solidity is closely integrated with Ethereum's infrastructure, and adheres to specific naming standards like ERC-20 and ERC-721, ensuring interoperability and functionality within the Ethereum ecosystem, features that are not paralleled in conventional programming languages.

## Solidity Syntax

We will delve into each specific solidity syntaxes which are pragma directive, contracts, state variables, functions, modifiers, events and lastly, fallback functions. These syntaxes are combined and build a complete smart contract.

### 1. Pragma Directive

- Solidity code typically begins with a pragma directive to specify the compiler version. This helps in preventing issues with future compiler versions that might introduce breaking changes.

```
pragma solidity ^0.8.0;
```

This line indicates that the code should be compiled using a compiler version equal to or greater than 0.8.0 but less than 0.9.0.

## 2. Contracts

- The primary building block in Solidity is a contract. A contract is similar to a class in object-oriented languages. It encapsulates data and functions that operate on that data.

```
contract MyContract {
        // State variables
        uint256 public myNumber;

        // Constructor
        constructor(uint256 initialNumber){
                myNumber = initialNumber;
        }

        // Function to update the number
        function updateNumber(uint256 newNumber) public {
                myNumber = newNumber;
        }
}
```

## 3. State Variables

- These are variables that permanently store data on the blockchain. They are declared within a contract. The stored location is called 'storage' where we have talked about three different saving locations in EVM which were storage, stack and memory.

```
uint256 public myNumber;
```

- The public keyword automatically generates a getter function for the variable.

## 4. Functions

- Functions in Solidity define the behavior of a contract. They can be called internally or by external entities.

```
function updateNumber(uint256 newNumber) public {
        myNumber = newNumber;
}
```

- The public keyword here specifies the visibility of the function.

## 5. Modifiers

- Modifiers are used to modify the behavior of functions in a declarative way. They are often used to enforce conditions before executing a function.

```
modifier onlyOwner(){
            require(msg,sender == owner, "Only the owner can call this
            function");
            _;
}
```

## 6. Events

- Events are used to log and notify external systems about specific actions within the contract.

```
event NumberUpdated(uint256 newNumber);
```

- They can be emitted inside functions.

```
function updateNumber(uint256 newNumber) public {
            myNumber = newNumber;
            emit NumberUpdated(newNumber);
}
```

## 7. Fallback Functions

- Solidity contracts can have a fallback function that is executed when a contract receives Ether without any specific function call.

```
contract FallbackExample{
            receive() external payable {
                        // Handle incoming Ether
            }
}
```

# Solidity by example

The best way to learn solidity is to visit the official site and see the actual document written by its creator. I've brought two good basic examples from "https://docs.soliditylang.org/".

Storage Example

```
// SPDX-License-Identifier: GPL-3.0
pragma solidity >=0.4.16 < 0.9.0;
contract SimpleStorage {
        uint storedData;

        function set(uint x) public {
                storedData = x;
        }

        function get() public view returns (uint) {
                return storedData;
        }
}
```

A contract in the sense of Solidity is a collection of code (its *functions*) and data (its *state*) that resides at a specific address on the Ethereum blockchain. The line uint storedData; declares a state variable called storedData of type uint (*unsigned integer of 256 bits*). You can think of it as a single slot in a database that you can query and alter by calling functions of the code that manages the database. In this example, the contract defines the functions set and get that can be used to modify or retrieve the value of the variable.

To access a member (like a state variable) of the current contract, you do not typically add the "this." prefix, you just access it directly via its name. Unlike in some other languages, omitting it is not just a matter of style, it results in a completely different way to access the member, but more on this later.

This contract does not do much yet apart from (due to the infrastructure built by Ethereum) allowing anyone to store a single number that is accessible by anyone in the world without a (feasible) way to prevent you from publishing this number. Anyone could call set again with a different value and overwrite your number, but the number is still stored in the history of the blockchain. Later, you will see how you can impose access restrictions so that only you can alter the number.

```solidity
// SPDX-License-Identifier: GPL-3.0
pragma solidity ^0.8.4;

contract Coin {
        // The keyword "public" makes variables
        // accessible from other contracts
        address public minter;
        mapping(address => uint) public balances;

        // Event allow clients to react to specific
        // contract changes you declare
        event Sent(address from, address to, uint amount);

        // Constructor code is only run when the contract
        // is created
        constructor() {
                minter = msg.sender;
        }

        // Sends an amount of newly created coins to an address
        // Can only be called by the contract creator
        function mint(address receiver, uint amount) public {
                require(msg.sender == minter);
                balances[receiver] += amount;
        }

        // Errors allow you to provide information about
        // why an operation failed. They are returned
        // to the caller of the function.
        error IndufficientBalance(uint requested, uint available);

        // Sends an amount of existing coins
        // from any caller to an address
        function send(address receiver, uint amount) public {
                if (amount > balances[msg.sender]){
                        revert InsufficientBalance({
                                requested: amount,
```

```
                                    available: balances[msg.sender]
                    });
        }

        balances[msg.sender] -= amount;
        balances[receiver] += amount;
        emit Sent(msg.sender, receiver, amount);
    }
}
```

This contract introduces some new concepts, let us go through them one by one. We will also take over the solidity syntax again for a recap!

The first line inside the "Coin" contract, address public minter, declares a state variable of type address. The address type is a 160-bit value that does not allow any arithmetic operations. It is suitable for storing addresses of contracts, or a hash of the public half of a keypair belonging to accounts.

The keyword public automatically generates a function that allows you to access the current value of the state variable from outside of the contract. Without this keyword, other contracts have no way to access the variable. The code of the function generated by the compiler is equivalent to the following (ignore external and view for now):

The next line, mapping(address => uint) public balances; also creates a public state variable, but it is a more complex data type. The mapping type maps addresses to unsigned integers.

Mappings can be seen as hash tables which are virtually initialized such that every possible key exists from the start and is mapped to a value whose byte-representation is all zeros. However, it is neither possible to obtain a list of all keys of a mapping, nor a list of all values. Record what you added to the mapping, or use it in a context where this is not needed. Or even better, keep a list, or use a more suitable data type.

The constructor is a special function that is executed during the creation of the contract and cannot be called afterwards. In this case, it permanently stores the address of the person creating the contract. The msg variable (together with tx and block) is a special global variable that contains properties which allow access to the blockchain. msg.sender is always the address where the current (external) function call came from.

The functions that make up the contract, and that users and contracts can call are mint and send. The mint function sends an amount of newly created coins to another address. The <require> function call defines conditions that revert all changes if not met. In this example, require(msg.sender == minter); ensures that only the creator of the contract can call mint. In general, the creator can mint as many tokens as they like, but at some point, this will lead to a phenomenon called "overflow". Note that because of the default Checked arithmetic, the transaction would revert if the expression balances[receiver] += amount; overflows, i.e., when balances[receiver] + amount in arbitrary precision arithmetic is larger than the maximum value of uint ($2^{256} - 1$). This is also true for the statement balances[receiver] += amount; in the function send.

"Errors" allow you to provide more information to the caller about why a condition or operation failed. Errors are used together with the <revert>. The revert statement unconditionally aborts and reverts all changes similar to the require function, but it also allows you to provide the name of an error and additional data which will be supplied to the caller (and eventually to the front-end application or block explorer) so that a failure can more easily be debugged or reacted upon.

The send function can be used by anyone (who already has some of these coins) to send coins to anyone else. If the sender does not have enough coins to send, the if condition evaluates to true. As a result, the revert will cause the operation to fail while providing the sender with error details using the InsufficientBalance error.

## Does EVM use solidity code directly?

```
contract Contract {
    function main() {
        memory[0x40:0x60] = 0x80;
        var var0 = msg.value;
        if (var0) { revert(memory[0x00:0x00]);}
        var0 = msg.sender;
        var var1 = 0x00;
        var var2 = 0x0100 ** var1;
        var var3 = storage[var];
        var var4 = var2;
    }
}
```

Contract Code

| ByteCode |
|---|
| 00:60 |
| 02:60 |
| 04:52 |
| 05:34 |
| 06:80 |
| 07:15 |
| 08:61 |

| Opcode |
|---|
| 00:PUSH1 |
| 02:PUSH1 |
| 04:MSTORE |
| 05:CALLVALUE |
| 06:DUP1 |
| 07:ISZERO |
| 08:PUSH2 |

*Contract code written in high level language(like solidity) is
compiled down to bytecode in order for EVM to understand it.*

Compilation in the context of the EVM involves translating high-level programming languages, like Solidity, into bytecode, a lower-level code that runs on the EVM. This process is crucial for ensuring platform independence, as the EVM operates across various hardware and software configurations in the Ethereum network. High-level code is easier for developers to write and understand but is typically platform-specific; converting it into bytecode enables it to be executed uniformly on any system running the EVM. This standardization is key to maintaining the decentralized and consistent operation of the Ethereum network.

Additionally, bytecode is more compact and efficient compared to high-level scripts, leading to quicker and more resource-efficient execution, which is vital in Ethereum's resource-limited blockchain environment. The compilation process also enhances security by potentially identifying vulnerabilities or errors beforehand. Furthermore, it ensures deterministic execution, a necessity for the blockchain to maintain a consistent state across all nodes. Each operation in the bytecode has a fixed gas cost, facilitating the calculation and limitation of gas consumption for smart contracts. These factors make compilation an essential step in preparing code for deployment in Ethereum's decentralized and constrained ecosystem.

# Chapter 4

# DeFi, NFT and DAOs

In this chapter we will learn the 3 pillars of blockchain's use cases in real life. Their identities are DeFi, NFT and DAO respectively. With the understanding of Bitcoin and Ethereum fundamentals and how the blockchain works, you would enjoy reading how people have implemented blockchain technology into various real-life fields. If you are really into blockchain technology, I recommend you to actually try some of the services or platforms which I used as an example in each section.

## DeFi

### Introduction to Decentralized Finance

In the realm of finance, a transformative wave is reshaping how we think about and interact with money, assets, and financial services. This wave is Decentralized Finance, commonly known as DeFi. DeFi represents a radical departure from traditional finance (TradFi), leveraging blockchain technology to decentralize and democratize financial services. Unlike the conventional financial system, which relies on centralized institutions like banks, stock exchanges, and insurance companies, DeFi operates on a peer-to-peer model, facilitated by smart contracts on blockchain networks. This innovation promises greater accessibility, transparency, and efficiency in financial transactions.

The limitations of traditional finance have been a catalyst for the rise of DeFi. TradFi, while foundational to our global economic infrastructure, is often criticized for its accessibility issues. A significant portion of the world's population remains unbanked or underbanked, lacking access to basic financial services. This problem is particularly acute in developing regions, where traditional banking infrastructure is sparse or non-existent. Moreover, TradFi is characterized by inefficiencies, such as high transaction fees and slow cross-border payment processing, stemming from the complex web of intermediaries involved in the financial ecosystem.

Centralization in TradFi also introduces systemic risks and vulnerabilities. The global financial crises of the past have starkly illustrated the dangers of over-reliance on central institutions. These crises exposed the fragility of a financial system hinged on a few centralized entities, prompting calls for a more resilient and inclusive financial architecture. DeFi emerges as a response to these challenges, offering an alternative where financial transactions are not controlled by any single entity but are instead distributed across a network of participants.

DeFi is not just a theoretical concept; it's a rapidly evolving field with real-world applications proliferating at an unprecedented pace. From lending and borrowing platforms to decentralized exchanges and stablecoins, DeFi is redefining the boundaries of financial services. However, this new frontier also brings its own set of challenges and complexities, which we will explore in depth in the following chapters. As we embark on this journey through the world of DeFi, we stand at the cusp of a financial revolution, one that promises to reshape our understanding of money, assets, and the very fabric of economic interactions.

## Blockchain and Smart Contracts in DeFi

At the core of blockchain's application in DeFi are smart contracts. Smart contracts automate and enforce the execution of contract terms, eliminating the need for intermediaries and reducing the potential for human error or manipulation. This automation is critical in DeFi, enabling a host of financial services such as lending, borrowing, trading, and yield farming to operate in a trustless environment where code essentially becomes the law.

In DeFi, smart contracts are utilized to create decentralized applications (DApps) that offer a variety of financial services. For example, in decentralized lending platforms, smart contracts allow users to lend or borrow cryptocurrencies without going through a traditional bank. The terms of the loan, including interest rates and duration, are embedded in the smart contract. Once agreed upon by the parties involved, the contract autonomously handles the distribution and repayment of funds, along with the accrual of interest.

Similarly, decentralized exchanges (DEXs) use smart contracts to facilitate peer-to-peer trading of cryptocurrencies without the need for a central authority to oversee trades. This not only enhances security by reducing the risk of hacks and fraud but also ensures transparency, as all transactions are recorded on the blockchain and are publicly verifiable.

## ERC-20

Before going into DeFi examples, let's see what ERC-20 is. The ERC-20 standard is a critical framework in the Ethereum blockchain, pivotal for creating fungible tokens via smart contracts. Proposed in 2015 by Fabian Vogelsteller, it has become integral for ensuring interoperability among various tokens within the Ethereum network.

Key features of ERC-20 tokens include their fungibility, meaning each token is identical and interchangeable, and their adherence to a standard set of rules governing functions like total supply, balance, and transfer methods. These tokens are managed by smart contracts, which automate and secure transactions on the Ethereum blockchain.

ERC-20 tokens have diverse applications, ranging from utility tokens within specific platforms to governance tokens that confer voting rights, as well as stablecoins tied to fiat currencies. They have also been instrumental in fundraising through Initial Coin Offerings (ICOs). It is crucial to understand what ERC-20 is since lots of tokens are minted as ERC-20 token standard to leverage Ethereum layer's advantages.

## Decentralized Exchanges (DEX)

Decentralized Exchanges (DEXs) are a key component of the Decentralized Finance ecosystem. They operate differently from traditional centralized exchanges (CEXs) by allowing users to conduct financial transactions directly with one another, without the need for an intermediary or central authority. This is made possible through the use of blockchain technology and smart contracts.

In a DEX, the trading process is facilitated by smart contracts, which are self-executing contracts with the terms of the agreement directly written into code. These smart contracts autonomously perform various functions such as order matching, trade execution, and the handling of funds. Unlike CEXs, where the exchange controls fund transfers and holds users' assets, in DEXs, users retain control of their private keys and therefore their assets, reducing the risk of theft from exchange hacks.

The logic behind DEXs is to create a trustless environment where users can safely trade cryptocurrencies without relying on an intermediary. This not only enhances security and privacy but also ensures transparency, as all transactions are recorded on the blockchain and are publicly verifiable.

Before going to real-world examples, let's go over one concept which is 'Slippage'. Slippage in cryptocurrency trading occurs when there is a difference between the expected price of a trade and the actual execution price. This is more common in the cryptocurrency market due to its high volatility and occasional low liquidity. The primary causes of slippage include rapid market movements that can occur in the volatile crypto space, large orders that significantly impact market prices, particularly in less liquid assets, and the inherent low liquidity in certain crypto markets or assets. These factors contribute to a wider bid-ask spread, increasing the likelihood and extent of slippage.

The impact of slippage on traders can be significant, often leading to higher costs for buyers and lower returns for sellers than initially anticipated. This is particularly relevant in high-volatility trades and when trading with leverage, where the effects of slippage can be magnified. To mitigate the risks and effects of slippage, traders commonly use limit orders, which allow for more control over the execution price, though with the risk that the order may not be fulfilled. Additionally, trading in more liquid markets or during peak hours can reduce the chances of slippage.

## UniSwap

Uniswap stands as a pioneering force in the world of Decentralized Finance (DeFi), renowned for its innovative approach to cryptocurrency trading. At its essence, Uniswap is a decentralized exchange (DEX) that operates on the Ethereum blockchain, facilitating automated trading of Ethereum and its various ERC-20 tokens.

*Order book matching system which we mostly see in TradFi(left). Neat interface of UniSwap, a platform where users could swap two different tokens in a low fee(right).*

An order book matching system relies on a list of buy and sell orders, matching buyers and sellers based on price and quantity, thereby operating on a supply and demand mechanism. This system often requires a third party or intermediary to facilitate these trades. In contrast, Uniswap uses an automated market maker (AMM) model, which eliminates the need for an order book. This allows for immediate and automated swaps without the need for matching individual buy and sell orders, significantly reducing reliance on traditional market makers and intermediaries.

*The infamous AMM logic is basically following x\*y=k rule for both swapped and swapping tokens. The fewer tokens there are in the liquidity pool, the more valuable the token is compared to the paired tokens.*

Uniswap revolutionizes cryptocurrency trading with its unique logic centered around an Automated Market Maker (AMM) system, diverging from traditional exchange models that rely on order books. Instead of matching buyers and sellers directly, Uniswap uses liquidity pools for each token pair, allowing users to trade against a pool of tokens. These pools are funded by liquidity providers who deposit their assets into the pool and, in return, receive liquidity tokens representing their share. Prices for trading pairs are determined algorithmically based on the relative balance of tokens in each pool, adhering to a simple formula that maintains the pool's overall balance. This design not only simplifies the trading process but also democratizes access to liquidity, allowing anyone to provide liquidity and earn fees, thereby fostering a more inclusive and efficient decentralized trading environment on the Ethereum blockchain.

Since its inception in 2018, Uniswap has rapidly grown to become one of the most widely used DEXs, often being credited for mainstreaming the concept of AMM. Its intuitive interface and trustless setup have lowered the barrier to entry for users looking to engage in decentralized trading. Beyond trading, Uniswap enables users to become liquidity providers by depositing their assets into shared pools. In return, they receive liquidity tokens, which represent their share of the pool and can be redeemed for a portion of the trading fees generated. The platform's emphasis on decentralization extends to governance as well, with UNI, Uniswap's native governance token, allowing holders to vote on key protocol decisions. The continuous evolution and upgrades, like Uniswap V3, reflect its commitment to improving efficiency, capital optimization, and offering enhanced control to liquidity providers. Uniswap's significant impact on the DeFi landscape is a testament to its innovative approach to decentralized trading and liquidity provision.

## Curve Finance

Curve Finance stands out in the DeFi landscape as a specialized DEX that primarily focuses on the trading of stablecoins(We will see what stablecoin is in the right next section). Launched in early 2020, Curve has carved a niche for itself by providing a platform for extremely efficient and low-cost stablecoin exchanges. The platform operates on the Ethereum blockchain and utilizes an AMM model, but with a unique twist tailored for stablecoins. Curve's AMM is designed to minimize slippage and maximize efficiency, a crucial feature for assets like stablecoins that are typically pegged to a specific value, such as the US dollar. This efficiency is achieved through a special pricing algorithm that reduces the deviation from the mean price, making Curve an attractive option for users looking to trade stablecoins with minimal transaction costs and little to no slippage.

Beyond stablecoin exchanges, Curve Finance has extended its offerings to include liquidity pools for various other types of tokens, particularly those representing the same underlying asset on different blockchains, known as wrapped tokens. This expansion addresses the growing need for cross-chain liquidity in the DeFi space. Curve's innovative approach also extends to its governance model, which is driven by its native token, CRV. Holders of CRV not only govern the protocol but also benefit from staking rewards and a boost in liquidity mining yields. Curve's liquidity pools are known for their high capital efficiency, making it a popular platform for yield farmers seeking optimal returns on their investments. As Curve continues to evolve, it remains at the forefront of DeFi innovation, particularly in the domain of stablecoin and cross-asset trading, reinforcing its position as a vital component of the decentralized finance ecosystem.

## Stable coin

*There are lots of stablecoin players in the DeFi space. BUSD, USDC, Tether, USTC, DAI from left to right accordingly. Source: pymnts*

A stablecoin is a type of cryptocurrency engineered to maintain a consistent value, contrasting with the typical volatility of digital currencies like Bitcoin and Ethereum. This stability is commonly achieved by pegging the stablecoin to a more stable asset, such as fiat currencies (e.g., the US Dollar or Euro) or commodities like gold. The aim is to combine the advantages of cryptocurrencies—such as digital, borderless transactions—with the reliability of a stable value, making stablecoins suitable for everyday transactions and reducing the financial risk for users.

There are three primary types of stablecoins: Fiat-Collateralized, Crypto-Collateralized, and Algorithmic. Fiat-Collateralized stablecoins are backed by a corresponding amount of a fiat currency, ensuring a stable value at a fixed ratio. Crypto-Collateralized stablecoins, on the other hand, use other cryptocurrencies as collateral, often over-collateralizing to accommodate the volatility of the crypto assets. Algorithmic stablecoins, devoid of any collateral, rely on algorithms to regulate their supply, adjusting it in response to market demand or price changes. These stablecoins are integral to the

DeFi ecosystem, providing a dependable medium for various financial activities.

You might be wondering how on earth the stablecoin issuer makes money with this? Actually, stablecoin issuers have various avenues for generating revenue, each capitalizing on the unique aspects of stablecoins and their role in digital finance. A primary source of income comes from the interest earned on reserves. These reserves, often consisting of fiat currencies, government bonds, or other assets, are the backbone of most stablecoins, particularly those that are fiat-collateralized. By investing these reserves in low-risk securities or lending them out, issuers can accumulate significant interest income. Additionally, transaction fees represent another revenue stream. While individual fees are usually low to maintain user engagement and competitive advantage, the sheer volume of transactions can lead to substantial cumulative earnings.

Other methods of revenue generation include seigniorage, especially for algorithmic stablecoins, and various financial services like lending, borrowing, and yield farming. These services not only provide direct income through interest rates and fees but also enhance the issuer's ecosystem, attracting more users and transactions. Integration with other blockchain projects and DeFi platforms can also be lucrative, as issuers may receive a part of the revenues or fees from these collaborations. For issuers with associated governance or utility tokens, appreciation in the value of these tokens can be a significant source of profit. Lastly, issuers can benefit from the spread in currency exchange rates when users convert between fiat and stablecoins, capitalizing on the fluctuations in the financial markets. The specific revenue model varies depending on the type of stablecoin and the issuer's policies, with operational costs and regulatory compliance also playing critical roles in their profitability.

## Tether(USDT)

Tether (USDT) is a type of cryptocurrency known as a stablecoin, which aims to keep its value stable by pegging it to a traditional fiat currency. Specifically, USDT is pegged to the value of the US Dollar, typically maintaining a 1:1 ratio, meaning one USDT is generally valued at one US Dollar. This pegging is achieved through the backing of USDT tokens with equivalent reserves of fiat currency, ensuring that for every USDT in circulation. This fiat-backed is handled by Tether Limited, the company behind Tether.

Tether was one of the first and has become one of the most widely used stablecoins in the cryptocurrency market. It plays a crucial role in providing stability and liquidity in the often volatile crypto markets. Traders and investors frequently use USDT as a means to hedge against the volatility of other cryptocurrencies, to move funds between different cryptocurrencies or platforms without converting back to traditional currency, and for engaging in trading activities on crypto exchanges that do not support traditional fiat currencies.

## Lending

In a DeFi lending platform, lenders provide their crypto assets to the platform's liquidity pool, from which borrowers can take out loans. Lenders earn interest on their assets, while borrowers pay interest on their loans. The interest rates are typically determined algorithmically, based on the supply and demand of the respective assets within the platform.

## Overcollaterilization

---

# Collateral Value > Loan Value

*Unlike in TradFi, DeFi does not have a credit loan, the lending platform should secure assets from the borrower that are greater than the loaned value. This prevents lending platforms for volatile risk in fluctuating crypto markets.*

One key aspect of DeFi lending is over-collateralization. Due to the absence of traditional credit checks and the pseudonymous nature of blockchain transactions, borrowers are often required to provide collateral (usually in the form of other cryptocurrencies) that exceeds the value of their loan.

In DeFi, liquidation occurs when the value of a borrower's collateral falls below a certain threshold, risking the solvency of their over-collateralized loan. DeFi platforms continuously monitor the loan-to-value (LTV) ratio, and if the collateral value drops significantly, triggering the liquidation threshold, part or all of the collateral is automatically sold, often through smart contracts, to repay the loan. This process, essential for maintaining platform stability, is facilitated by liquidators who are incentivized to repay under-collateralized loans in exchange for discounted collateral. Borrowers face liquidation penalties, adding to the loan repayment to cover the associated risks. This automated system ensures speed and efficiency in managing the inherent volatility and risk in the crypto market.

DeFi lending platforms offer several advantages over traditional lending. They provide easy access to credit and a passive income stream for lenders, often with higher interest rates than traditional savings accounts. They also offer transparency, as all transactions are recorded on the blockchain, and inclusivity, as they are accessible to anyone with an internet connection, regardless of geographic location or credit history.

## Maker DAO

Maker DAO is a prominent project in the DeFi ecosystem, best known for its development and maintenance of the Dai (DAI) stablecoin. Launched in 2017 on the Ethereum blockchain, Maker DAO represents a decentralized autonomous organization (DAO) that operates through smart contracts and community governance.

The core of Maker DAO's innovation is the Dai stablecoin, which is pegged to the US Dollar but is not backed by fiat currency in a bank account. Instead, it maintains its peg through a system of collateralized debt positions (CDPs), now called Vaults in the Maker Protocol.

For a brief explanation of what Collateralized Debt Positions (CDPs), they are a financial mechanism used primarily in the world of decentralized finance (DeFi), particularly in platforms that enable users to generate stablecoins. In a CDP, a user locks up cryptocurrency as collateral in a smart contract to borrow against it, usually in the form of a stablecoin. This system allows users to leverage their cryptocurrency holdings to generate liquidity without selling their assets. The collateral ensures the stability and security of the debt, as the value of the collateral typically exceeds the value of the loan. If the value of the collateral falls below a certain threshold, the CDP can be liquidated to cover the debt, protecting the system's integrity.

Back to Maker DAO, users can generate Dai by depositing collateral assets (like ETH or other supported cryptocurrencies) into these Vaults. The system ensures that the value of the collateral always exceeds the value of Dai issued, maintaining over-collateralization to stabilize Dai's value.

Maker DAO's ecosystem is governed by its holders of its governance token, MKR. MKR token holders have the right to vote on various proposals that determine the rules and parameters of the Maker Protocol, such as which types of collateral can be used, risk parameters, stability fees (interest rates), and other system modifications. This decentralized governance model allows for a community-driven approach to managing the stability and functionality of the Dai stablecoin.

## Yield farming and Liquidity Mining

Yield Farming, is a practice where users lock up or 'stake' their crypto assets in a DeFi protocol to earn additional rewards, usually in the form of cryptocurrency. Yield farmers move their assets around different DeFi protocols and strategies to maximize their return on investment. These returns come from various sources including interest from lenders, trading fees from being part of a liquidity pool, or rewards in the form of additional tokens.

The mechanics of yield farming can get quite complex, involving various strategies like leveraging (borrowing funds to amplify returns), participating in different liquidity pools, and using various DeFi platforms. The rewards are often paid out in the platform's native token, and the overall yield is typically calculated annually as a percentage yield (APY).

*Yield farmers find the maximum strategy by analyzing all the possible sources they could accommodate! Source: finematics*

Liquidity Mining is a subset of yield farming, where users provide liquidity to a DeFi protocol, particularly to a decentralized exchange, by depositing a pair of tokens in a liquidity pool. In return, these liquidity providers (LPs) earn rewards. These rewards can be in the form of transaction fees generated by the underlying DeFi platform or new tokens issued by the protocol. Liquidity mining is crucial in ensuring there is enough liquidity on a DEX to facilitate trading without large price slippage.

One of the key attractions of liquidity mining is the distribution of new tokens – it is often used as a mechanism by DeFi projects to incentivize users to supply liquidity to their platforms. This distribution can significantly enhance the returns for liquidity providers, especially if the value of the distributed tokens appreciates over time.

## Yearn.finance

Yearn.finance revolutionizes the way users earn interest on their cryptocurrency holdings by automating yield farming. Operating on the Ethereum blockchain, it strategically reallocates users' deposited funds across various lending protocols like Aave and Compound to secure the best possible returns. This process is managed by smart contracts, ensuring efficiency and optimization. Furthermore, Yearn's Vaults, which are pools of funds with dedicated yield-maximizing strategies, allow users to deposit their tokens and receive yTokens (such as yUSD, yETH) in return, representing their share in these Vaults. These strategies, encompassing activities like lending and liquidity provision, are community-driven and subject to governance votes.

The governance of Yearn.finance is notably decentralized, facilitated through its native token, YFI. Holders of YFI have voting rights on key protocol decisions, encompassing new strategies and modifications to the platform. This approach underlines Yearn's commitment to community-led development and decentralization.

## Derivatives

Derivatives in DeFi are financial instruments whose value is derived from underlying assets like cryptocurrencies, fiat currencies, or other financial indicators. DeFi derivatives platforms offer a wide range of instruments, including options, futures, swaps, and synthetic assets, enabling users to engage in risk management, speculation, and gain diverse asset exposure.

A notable feature in DeFi derivatives is the perpetual contract, commonly known as "perpetual" or "perp". But wait, let's learn what futures are in derivatives before talking about perpetual contracts. Futures, a fundamental type of derivative, are financial contracts obligating the buyer to purchase, and the seller to sell, a specific asset, such as commodities, stocks, or currencies, at a predetermined future date and price. Unlike options, which provide the right but not the obligation to buy or sell the asset, futures contracts impose a legal obligation on both parties to fulfill the terms of the contract at expiration. The price of the future is determined by the underlying asset's market price, and these contracts are typically traded on exchanges. Futures are used for hedging against price movements, speculating on the future value of assets, or managing financial risk, offering the advantage of leveraging investments while also introducing the potential for significant losses if the market moves unfavorably relative to the contract terms.

In the case of perpetual contracts, they are similar to traditional futures but with no expiration date, allowing traders to hold positions indefinitely. This adds considerable flexibility compared to standard futures. The pricing of perpetuals is kept in line with the underlying asset through a funding rate mechanism, which is periodically adjusted and paid between long and short positions. Perpetuals in DeFi often offer high leverage, enabling traders to amplify their potential gains. However, this also escalates the risk, as losses are equally magnified.

Besides perpetual trading, there is another type of trading which is 'Spot trading' in the DeFi scene. Spot trading is immediate buying and selling of assets for instant settlement, where the transfer of assets and payment occurs almost simultaneously. Its primary goal is to exploit short-term market price movements, allowing traders and investors to profit from the difference in buying and selling prices over brief periods. This form of trading is crucial for both individual and institutional participants, offering a direct and efficient way to capitalize on market fluctuations. Additionally, spot trading is instrumental in price discovery, as it provides real-time insight into supply and demand dynamics, thereby helping determine fair market prices. The prices from spot trades also serve as benchmarks for various derivative products and financial instruments, playing a significant role in the overall market valuation of cryptocurrencies. Spot trading, therefore, not only facilitates immediate and efficient trade execution but also contributes significantly to the broader financial market's functioning.

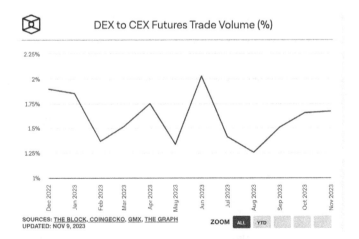

*Derivative trading volume of DEX/CEX ratio in DeFi. It is maintaining a low percentage of 1.5%~2%, opening a high potential of DEX derivative platforms.*

Even though derivatives take over the huge trading volume over spot trading, the ratio of derivative trade volume of DEX/CEX maintains less than 2% at the time of november, 2023. Since CEXs generally offer greater liquidity, more advanced technological infrastructure, and sophisticated risk management tools that are crucial for derivatives trading. They also have the advantage of regulatory compliance, which can attract a broader range of traders. Additionally, the established brand recognition and user trust in CEXs, along with their ease of use and efficiency, make them more appealing, especially for complex financial products like derivatives.

However, the potential of DEX derivatives lies in their ability to offer a trustless and permissionless trading environment, which is a significant shift from the traditional finance sector. Decentralized derivatives platforms can potentially lower entry barriers, reduce counterparty risks, and offer a higher degree of transparency and security through smart contracts. This could lead to more inclusive financial markets, where a broader range of participants can access complex financial products without the need for intermediaries.

## GMX

GMX is a decentralized platform offering both spot and perpetual exchange services, allowing traders to open long or short positions on major cryptocurrencies. Unique to GMX is its use of a single multi-asset liquidity pool called GLP, which consists of various assets such as stablecoins, Wrapped Bitcoin, and Wrapped Ethereum. Liquidity providers in this pool mint GLP tokens and earn a significant portion (70%) of all trading fees on the platform. GMX's innovation lies in its combination of decentralized finance (DeFi) principles with traditional trading mechanisms, specifically perpetual contracts, a popular derivative in financial markets.

In terms of tokenomics, GMX has two primary tokens: the GMX governance token and the GLP liquidity provider token. The GMX token, with a capped supply of 13.25 million, is used for governance and staking, providing holders with various rewards, including escrowed GMX tokens and a portion of trading fees. The GLP token, in contrast, is backed by the pool's assets and entitles holders to a share of the platform's trading fees and profits. This dual-token structure supports the platform's decentralized governance and incentivizes participation and liquidity provision.

GMX distinguishes itself in the DeFi space by providing low swap fees and minimal price impact trades, enabling traders to manage large positions efficiently. The platform operates on both the Arbitrum and Avalanche blockchains, though it's important to note that GLP tokens on these two networks are not interoperable. With its innovative approach to perpetual contracts and liquidity provision, GMX has garnered significant interest and participation in the cryptocurrency derivatives market, reflecting the growing demand for decentralized financial services.

## Liquidity staking

Liquidity staking, or Liquid Staking, in DeFi is a process that enhances the utility of staked assets in blockchain networks. It allows cryptocurrency holders to engage in staking, which is fundamental to the security and consensus of Proof of Stake (PoS) networks, while retaining the liquidity of their assets. This is facilitated through the issuance of Liquid Staking Derivatives (LSDs)(don't get confused with the Lysergic acid diethylamide, also short for LSD, a hallucinogens drug!!), which are tokenized representations of the staked cryptocurrencies, including the accrued staking rewards. These LSDs enable holders to utilize their staked assets in various DeFi protocols without needing to unstake, thereby maintaining their liquidity and active participation in the network.

In addition to LSDs, there are Liquid Staking Tokens (LSTs), which serve a similar purpose. These tokens are fungible and act as a stand-in for the staked assets, representing the ownership and rights associated with the staking process. Holders of LSTs can trade, lend, or use these tokens across the DeFi ecosystem, which allows them to unlock the value of their staked assets without withdrawing from the staking process. This feature is particularly beneficial for users who want to optimize their asset utility and engage in multiple yield-generating activities simultaneously.

However, despite the apparent benefits of liquidity staking in terms of capital efficiency and liquidity, it comes with its own set of challenges and risks. The primary concern revolves around the value and stability of the derivative tokens (LSDs or LSTs), which depend on the credibility and stability of the issuing platforms. Additionally, like all DeFi activities, liquidity staking is subject to risks associated with smart contract vulnerabilities and the overall solvency of the platforms involved. As such, while liquidity staking presents an innovative solution in the DeFi space, addressing the liquidity constraints of traditional staking, users need to be cautious and informed about the specific platforms and protocols they choose to engage with.

## Lido finance

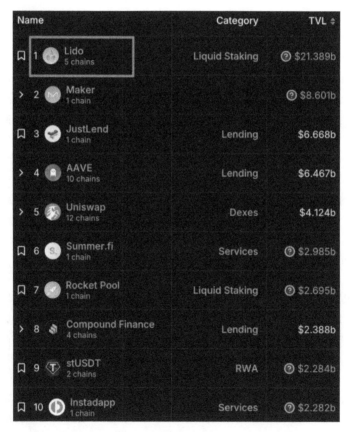

| Name | Category | TVL ↕ |
|---|---|---|
| □ 1 Lido — 5 chains | Liquid Staking | ⑦ $21.389b |
| > 2 Maker — 1 chain | | ⑦ $8.601b |
| □ 3 JustLend — 1 chain | Lending | $6.668b |
| > 4 AAVE — 10 chains | Lending | $6.467b |
| > 5 Uniswap — 12 chains | Dexes | $4.124b |
| □ 6 Summer.fi — 1 chain | Services | ⑦ $2.985b |
| □ 7 Rocket Pool — 1 chain | Liquid Staking | ⑦ $2.695b |
| > 8 Compound Finance — 4 chains | Lending | $2.388b |
| □ 9 stUSDT — 2 chains | RWA | ⑦ $2.284b |
| □ 10 Instadapp — 1 chain | Services | ⑦ $2.282b |

*Lido finance is ranked the top TVL(Total Value Locked) among all of the DeFi protocols, winning by overwhelming value from the 2nd(MakerDAO).*

Lido Finance is a DeFi protocol, primarily focused on providing liquidity solutions for staked assets in the Ethereum ecosystem. It addresses the key issue of illiquidity faced by participants in Ethereum 2.0 staking, wherein staked ETH is locked and inaccessible. By staking with Lido, users don't have to worry about the minimum staking requirements(which is 32 ETH) or the complexities of running a validator node.

Through liquidity staking, Lido allows users to stake ETH and receive stETH tokens in return, representing their staked ETH and the accumulated rewards. These stETH tokens maintain liquidity and can be actively traded or used across various DeFi applications, offering flexibility and utility in the broader DeFi space.

The governance of Lido Finance is orchestrated by the Lido Decentralized Autonomous Organization (DAO), which involves LDO token holders in decision-making processes. Launched in January 2021, the LDO token is an Ethereum-native ERC-20 token, functioning as a governance token that enables holders to vote on proposals and shape the future of the protocol. The Lido ecosystem comprises several components, including a network of selected node operators responsible for validating transactions and maintaining the security of the Ethereum network. This makes staking accessible to a wider audience, allowing users with limited technical expertise to participate in Ethereum staking.

Lido Finance stands out for its integration with the DeFi ecosystem and its ability to simplify the staking process. By tokenizing staked assets through stETH, it provides a tangible solution to the liquidity constraints of traditional staking methods in Ethereum 2.0. The Lido DAO and its governance model further enhance this, allowing for a decentralized and community-driven approach to protocol management and development.

# Oracles

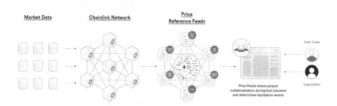

*Chainlink is the leading company in oracle space in crypto. It aggregates data from numerous platforms, making it both trustful and decentralized.*

Oracles provide a crucial link between blockchain-based smart contracts and external, real-world data. Smart contracts, by their design, are restricted to the blockchain's internal data and cannot access or interact with external information independently. This limitation is significant for DeFi applications that require up-to-date and accurate information from the real world, such as current market prices, interest rates, or other relevant data. Oracles address this gap by acting as third-party services that fetch necessary external data and feed it into the blockchain, enabling smart contracts to function based on this information.

The necessity of oracles in DeFi stems from the need for real-world data to facilitate various operations. For instance, DeFi applications like synthetic assets, derivatives, and stablecoins depend on accurate, real-time data from external sources to function correctly. Oracles provide this data, ensuring that smart contracts can execute decisions based on timely and accurate information. Moreover, the security and trustworthiness of oracles are crucial, as the integrity of data they provide directly impacts the reliability and safety of DeFi platforms. Inaccurate or manipulated data fed into a smart contract can lead to incorrect execution of contract terms, potentially resulting in significant financial losses.

In practice, oracles are utilized in DeFi for a variety of purposes. They supply real-time price feeds to decentralized exchanges, lending platforms, and prediction markets, and provide updates on changing market conditions, enabling DeFi platforms to respond dynamically, such as initiating collateral liquidation processes. Oracles also find use in decentralized insurance applications, where they can trigger payments based on verified real-world events.

However, the reliance on oracles introduces potential vulnerabilities, especially when they are centralized, as it raises concerns about data accuracy and manipulation - known as the "oracle problem". To mitigate these risks, many DeFi projects employ multiple oracles or use decentralized oracle networks to enhance data integrity and security. This approach underscores the importance of oracles in DeFi while highlighting the need for careful integration to ensure the overall reliability and safety of DeFi applications.

## Tokenomics in DeFi

*Token distribution of Near protocol. One of the fastest ways to skim tokenomics is to look at the token distribution diagram. Source: Near protocol*

Tokenomics in DeFi encompasses the economic aspects of a cryptocurrency within its ecosystem, including token distribution, utility, governance, and supply dynamics. This concept is fundamental in defining a token's practical use, value, and sustainability in the market. The supply of a token, both maximum and circulating, is crucial in determining its scarcity and market availability. For example, Bitcoin's fixed supply contrasts with Ethereum's increasing supply. The utility of a token, such as its role in governance, staking, or as a medium of exchange, significantly impacts user adoption and demand.

The initial distribution and allocation of tokens are pivotal for DeFi projects. Methods like token sales, airdrops, and ICOs are common for distribution. The fair allocation among stakeholders, including the project team, advisors, investors, and community, is essential for trust and aligning interests. Additionally, vesting schedules for tokens help stabilize the market by preventing sudden price drops due to oversupply. Incentive mechanisms, varying across different blockchain consensus models like PoW and PoS, play a role in encouraging network participation, such as rewarding miners in PoW or validators in PoS for their contributions.

Token burning, the process of permanently removing tokens from circulation, is a strategy employed by some projects to enhance token scarcity and potential value. This, along with governance features where token holders have voting rights on project decisions, decentralizes control and aligns stakeholder interests with the project's success. Effective tokenomics balance these elements to foster a thriving ecosystem, as exemplified by successful DeFi projects like AAVE and Uniswap. On the contrary, poorly managed tokenomics can lead to price instability, control centralization, or even project failure.

Several DeFi projects exemplify diverse tokenomic models. MakerDAO, with its dual-token system (MKR and DAI), offers governance rights through MKR and maintains DAI as a stablecoin. The value of MKR is intrinsically linked to the protocol's performance, with tokens being burned as fees are paid, aligning the interests of holders with the health of the platform. Compound's COMP token is used for governance, giving holders a say in key protocol decisions like adding new cryptocurrencies or adjusting platform rules. Its distribution to users fosters participation and decentralizes control. Uniswap's UNI token, allocated to past protocol users via an airdrop, serves a similar governance function, demonstrating a commitment to decentralization and community involvement.

Understanding tokenomics is essential for participants in the DeFi space, be they developers, investors, or users. It offers critical insights into the health and future prospects of DeFi projects, highlighting the importance of balanced and well-thought-out economic models. This understanding is key to navigating the dynamic and often complex world of decentralized finance, enabling informed decisions and participation in this evolving sector.

## Regulatory landscape and DeFi hacks

The regulatory landscape for DeFi presents unique challenges due to its inherent characteristics of decentralization, global operation, and the pseudonymity of blockchain transactions. Jurisdictional issues arise as DeFi platforms do not conform to traditional geographical boundaries, making the application of national regulations complex.

Additionally, the decentralized and often anonymous nature of these platforms complicates efforts to ensure consumer protection and compliance with traditional financial regulatory standards. Ensuring the safety of consumers against fraud and market manipulation, typically addressed in conventional finance, becomes challenging in a DeFi context where there's no central authority to oversee and regulate activities.

Regulatory bodies also face difficulties in implementing Anti-Money Laundering (AML) and Know Your Customer (KYC) protocols within the DeFi space. The pseudonymous nature of blockchain transactions raises concerns about the potential misuse of DeFi for illicit activities, yet enforcing AML and KYC standards is not straightforward in a decentralized setting. Moreover, taxation and financial reporting in the realm of DeFi add another layer of complexity, as the diverse range of transactions and the borderless nature of these platforms challenge traditional tax categorization and compliance processes.

In response to these challenges, regulators are beginning to develop frameworks specifically tailored to DeFi, with an emphasis on securities laws, AML/CFT(Combating the Financial of Terrorism) regulations, and consumer protection guidelines. This involves dialogue and collaboration with DeFi developers, industry experts, and community members, aiming to create informed and balanced regulations that support innovation while mitigating inherent risks. A key focus for regulators is understanding how to apply rules designed for centralized entities to DeFi's decentralized model, particularly in terms of assigning responsibility and compliance within decentralized structures like DAOs. As the DeFi sector continues to evolve, regulatory approaches are expected to be adaptive, evolving alongside technological and market developments.

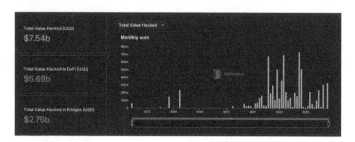

*Total $7.54b was hacked in DeFi space by the end of 2023. Source: DeFiLlama*

The DeFi sector has experienced several significant hacks, emphasizing the critical importance of security in this rapidly evolving field. Among the most notable is the Poly Network hack of August 2021, where over $600 million was stolen, marking it as one of the largest DeFi thefts. The hacker exploited a vulnerability in the cross-chain interoperability protocol but later started returning the funds. Another major incident occurred with Compound Finance in October 2021, where a bug in its Comptroller contract inadvertently led to the distribution of about $150 million worth of COMP tokens. Cream Finance faced multiple attacks, losing millions due to vulnerabilities in its system. Similarly, BadgerDAO suffered a substantial loss of around $120 million in December 2021 due to a front-end attack.

Other significant breaches include the Wormhole Bridge hack in February 2022, resulting in the theft of around $320 million, and the Ronin Network hack in March 2022, where about $625 million was stolen. These attacks, often involving the exploitation of smart contract vulnerabilities or security oversights, highlight the persistent challenges of ensuring robust security in DeFi platforms. They underscore the need for more stringent security measures, comprehensive audits, and improved risk management practices to safeguard assets in the DeFi space. As DeFi continues to grow, addressing these security vulnerabilities remains a crucial focus for developers, users, and regulatory bodies.

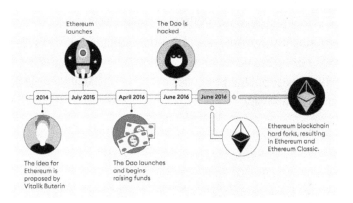

*Behind the birth of Ethereum Classic, there was a
tragic hack of "The DAO". Source: Bitpanda*

"The DAO" was a pioneering venture within the Ethereum blockchain ecosystem, launched in April 2016. Designed as a decentralized venture capital fund, it allowed investors to contribute Ether (Ethereum's cryptocurrency) in exchange for DAO tokens, granting them voting rights on project funding. This model was groundbreaking, not only for its substantial fundraising success—over $150 million in Ether—but also for its innovative approach to investment and governance. The DAO embodied the principles of decentralization and collective decision-making, marking a significant shift from traditional, centralized venture capital methods.

However, "The DAO" faced a major crisis in June 2016 due to a critical vulnerability in its smart contract code. An attacker exploited this flaw, known as a "reentrancy bug," to repeatedly withdraw large amounts of Ether into a subsidiary account before the main contract could update its balance. This led to the loss of about $50 million, one-third of The DAO's funds. The incident not only resulted in a considerable financial loss but also significantly impacted the Ethereum community, causing a steep decline in Ether's value and raising serious concerns about the security of smart contracts.

In response to the hack, the Ethereum community took a controversial step by implementing a hard fork, effectively reversing the transaction history to a point before the attack. This decision, while successful in recovering the stolen funds, led to a split in the Ethereum blockchain, resulting in two separate chains: Ethereum (ETH), which adopted the fork, and Ethereum Classic (ETC), which maintained the original chain. The DAO hack and the subsequent fork became a watershed moment in the cryptocurrency world, emphasizing the need for enhanced security in smart contracts and sparking debates about the principles of immutability and decentralization in blockchain technology.

# NFT

## What is a NFT

*CryptoPunks are 24x24 pixel art images, generated algorithmically. Most are punky-looking guys and girls, but there are a few rarer types mixed in(left). THE BORED APE YACHT CLUB, a limited NFT collection where the token itself doubles as your membership to a swamp club for apes(right)*

Do you remember the NFT craze that hit 2021? There were a lot of new riches born not only from the coin investment, but also from trading NFTs which were insanely soaring in prices at that moment. Some leading projects like Cryptopunks and Board apes' art value were traded at more than $20M dollars at the peak of the NFT boom.

Even though the sales value of NFT by the end of 2023 has shrinked more than 95% from the peak month in 2021, NFT is still an important sector in understanding the use cases of blockchain. Let's see what NFT really is, how it secures the originality of the art work, how to make one and how it is used now.

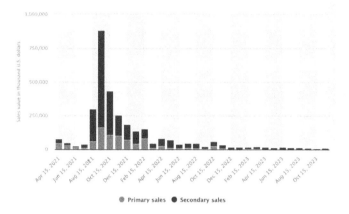

*Sales value in thousand U.S. dollars of NFT(21.4 ~ 23.11)*

NFTs, or Non-Fungible Tokens, are digital assets built on blockchain technology. It has emerged as a groundbreaking concept, capturing the attention of diverse groups from artists and collectors to investors and technologists. Unlike traditional digital items, NFTs introduce a unique sense of ownership and exclusivity, reshaping how value and authenticity are perceived in the digital world.

NFTs, at their essence, are digital assets that signify ownership or proof of authenticity of a unique item or content, anchored in blockchain technology. Distinct from cryptocurrencies like Bitcoin or Ethereum, which are fungible and exchangeable on a one-to-one basis, NFTs are irreplaceable and non-interchangeable, attributing to them a unique value proposition. This uniqueness is characterized by three key aspects.

First, each NFT contains specific metadata and attributes, recorded on the blockchain, ensuring no two NFTs are identical. This is akin to the distinctiveness found in art pieces, where no two works are exactly alike.

Second, each NFT is distinct, characterized by a unique identifier that sets it apart from other tokens. This non-fungibility is central to their value, as it ensures that each NFT represents a specific, one-of-a-kind asset.

Unlike cryptocurrencies, which are divisible, NFTs are typically indivisible, meaning they exist as whole items—you either own the entire token or none of it. This is crucial for representing unique digital or physical assets.

And lastly, NFTs offer a transparent and immutable record of ownership and transaction history. This transparency is vital for verifying the provenance of digital items, allowing for the confirmation of the history and originality of an NFT. It marks a significant shift in digital ownership, making NFTs an invaluable tool in the digital era.

## ERC-721 & ERC-1155

ERC-721 and ERC-1155 have emerged as foundational Ethereum token standards, each playing a crucial role in shaping the NFT landscape. ERC-721, known as the pioneer of NFT standards, was the first to facilitate the creation, transfer, and tracking of unique digital assets on the Ethereum blockchain. Its primary strength lies in its ability to ensure the uniqueness and indivisibility of each token, making it ideal for digital collectibles and art. This standard has been pivotal in popularizing NFTs, providing a robust framework for transparent ownership and provenance tracking, and ensuring interoperability across various platforms.

ERC-1155, developed to address some limitations of ERC-721, introduced a more flexible and efficient approach. Unlike ERC-721, which is limited to non-fungible tokens, ERC-1155 supports both fungible and non-fungible tokens within a single contract. This multi-token standard allows for batch transfers of various token types, significantly reducing transaction costs and enhancing efficiency. ERC-1155's reduced storage requirements and optimized smart contract logic make it particularly advantageous in gaming and virtual worlds where a combination of fungible and non-fungible assets are common.

The choice between ERC-721 and ERC-1155 depends on the specific needs of a project. ERC-721 is well-suited for assets requiring unique identification, while ERC-1155 offers greater versatility for environments involving diverse token interactions. Both standards have facilitated the growth of digital collectibles and art, providing a foundation for future innovations in digital asset applications.

## NFT trading platforms

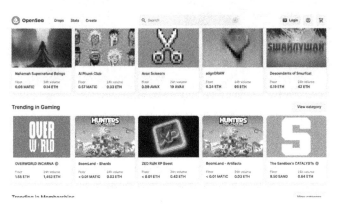

*OpenSea is the most famous platform for buying, selling and trading NFT. Source: OpenSea*

OpenSea is the most famous platform in the NFT marketplace, specialized in the buying, selling, and discovery of Non-Fungible Tokens. It supports a vast array of NFT categories, including digital art, collectibles, domain names, and virtual real estate. The platform is primarily built on the Ethereum blockchain, adhering to the ERC-721 and ERC-1155 standards essential for NFT transactions, and is known for its user-friendly interface. This accessibility makes it appealing to both novices and experienced users in the blockchain space. OpenSea also offers features for minting NFTs, allowing creators to easily tokenize and sell their work.

Key aspects of OpenSea include its auction and fixed-price sales mechanisms, community engagement tools, and integration with various digital wallets, enhancing its functionality and user experience. The platform ensures secure and transparent transactions through its decentralized blockchain framework, emphasizing security in digital asset transfers. Additionally, it supports royalty payments for creators, providing them with a revenue stream from secondary sales. OpenSea's role in the NFT ecosystem is significant, serving as a comprehensive hub for creators, collectors, and traders in the digital asset space.

*Blur is an innovative platform which applies an order
book matching system for trading NFTs.*

Blur is a NFT marketplace that launched in October 2022 and quickly established itself as a major player, challenging industry giants like OpenSea. Built on the Ethereum blockchain, Blur's approach is tailored for advanced NFT traders, offering features like faster NFT snipe and sweep, real-time price feeds, and sophisticated portfolio management tools. Its aggregation of NFTs from various sources including OpenSea, Rarible, and SuperRare, coupled with its zero trading fees for NFT sales, has helped it gain significant traction in the market. The platform is known for its speed, unique listing options, analytics, and efficient sweeping functionality.

Central to Blur's ecosystem is its native ERC-20 $BLUR token, with a total supply of 3 billion tokens, of which 51% is allocated to the community. This token allows holders to participate in governance decisions, impacting the platform's development. Additionally, Blur has implemented a decentralized autonomous organization (DAO) to further decentralize decision-making and empower its community. With its focus on professional traders and innovative features, Blur stands out as a formidable competitor in the NFT marketplace landscape, offering a unique blend of speed, efficiency, and community-driven governance.

## How to mint a NFT?

NFTs are governed by smart contracts on the blockchain. These are self-executing contracts with the terms of the agreement written into code, which automate the process of verification, enforcement, and execution of transactions. These contracts also define the NFT's properties, like ownership and transferability.

The metadata of an NFT provides information about the asset, such as its creator, history, and authenticity, often stored off-chain due to blockchain storage constraints. Services like the InterPlanetary File System (IPFS) are used for off-chain storage, linking the on-chain token to its digital asset securely. Owning NFT means holding the private key to the wallet where it's stored, serving as proof of ownership. The blockchain's record-keeping ensures the provenance and authenticity of the NFT, recording its entire history, including creation, sales, and transfers. This interoperability across platforms is a key feature, thanks to the use of standard protocols like ERC-721.

```solidity
// SPDX-License-Identifier: MIT
pragma solidity ^0.8.0;

import "@openzeppelin/contracts/token/ERC721/ERC721.sol";
import "@openzeppelin/contracts/utils/Counters.sol";

contract EmotionalShapes is ERC721 {
    using Counters for Counters.Counter;
    Counters.Counter private _tokenIdCounter;

    constructor() ERC721("EmotionalShapes", "ESS") {}
    function _baseURI() internal pure override returns (string memory) {
        return "https://YOUR_API/api/erc721/";
    }

    function mint(address to) public returns (uint256) {
        require(_tokenIdCounter.current() < 3);
        _tokenIdCounter.increment();
        _safeMint(to, _tokenIdCounter.current());

        return _tokenIdCounter.current();
    }
}
```

*It only requires 14 lines of code to mint your own brand new NFT!!*

The above code is a smart contract written in solidity. It shows how simple it is to write a contract to mint a new coin! There is a thankful method we can use to help. It is "OpenZeppelin" which is a set of pre-written code blocks or functions in solidity. This has already made an implementation of ERC-721 which is a kind of boiler-template of minting a NFT.

Actually, there are lots of NFT platforms which do this minting procedure automatically so there is no need for you to write it manually. But if you are a coding geek, I won't stop you!

Now it's time to actually mint a NFT. Let's follow this step-by-step guidance and mint your own NFT.

1. **Choose Your Digital Asset**: Decide what digital item (art, music, video) you want to turn into a NFT.
2. **Select a Blockchain**: Choose a blockchain that supports NFTs, like Ethereum, Binance Smart Chain, or Polygon.
3. **Create a Digital Wallet**: Set up a digital wallet that supports NFTs and the chosen blockchain.
4. **Buy Cryptocurrency**: Purchase cryptocurrency (like ETH for Ethereum) for paying transaction fees.
5. **Select a NFT Marketplace**: Choose a platform (like OpenSea, Rarible) where you will mint the NFT.
6. **Upload Your Asset:** Upload your digital file to the marketplace.
7. **Mint the NFT**: Follow the platform's process to create your NFT, which involves linking your digital file to a new blockchain entry.
8. **List or Sell the NFT**: Once minted, you can list your NFT for sale on the marketplace.

# What comprises NFT?

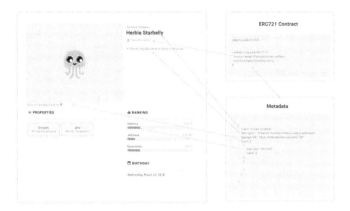

*Metadata in NFT. Source: OpenSea*

What components does NFT have? You might be surprised to find out there are lots of additional information in the NFT besides the art data. An NFT comprises several key components: a unique identifier that distinguishes it from other tokens, metadata providing details such as title and creator, the digital asset it represents (like art or music), a smart contract on the blockchain dictating its properties and rules, ownership records indicating its transaction history and current owner, and a link to where the digital asset is stored, often on a decentralized platform like IPFS. These elements together make up the structure and functionality of an NFT.

*Traits(properties) window of specific NFT. Source: OpenSea*

There is also an interesting component in NFT which is called "traits". Traits in NFTs refer to the characteristics or attributes that define and differentiate each NFT within a collection. These traits can include visual aspects like color, shape, accessories, and more in the case of digital art, or they could pertain to specific properties or abilities for NFTs used in digital games.

The rarity and uniqueness of certain traits often influence the value and desirability of an NFT, making those with rarer traits more sought after by collectors and enthusiasts. For example, the 'Alien' variety of CryptoPunks has only nine known instances, making them exceptionally rare and valuable. One such Alien Punk sold for over $7.5 million in early 2021, showcasing the immense value attributed to rare traits.

## Trading fees in NFT

In the NFT (Non-Fungible Token) market, trading fees are a vital component, encompassing a range of charges incurred during different stages of an NFT's lifecycle. Firstly, there are minting fees, paid when an NFT is created or 'minted' on the blockchain. These fees compensate for the computational resources required for processing and validating the transaction. They vary based on the blockchain platform and its current network traffic. Additionally, some marketplaces might charge listing fees for placing an NFT on sale, although major platforms like OpenSea usually waive these fees to attract more users.

Another significant aspect of NFT trading fees is transaction costs, commonly referred to as "gas fees." These are necessary for all blockchain transactions and are paid to network validators or miners for their service in processing transactions. The cost is influenced by the network's demand and congestion at the time of the transaction. Furthermore, NFT marketplaces typically earn revenue through platform commissions, taking a percentage of each sale. For instance, OpenSea charges a commission of 2.5% per transaction. This commission model is the primary revenue source for these platforms.

Finally, NFTs introduce a unique concept in digital asset trading: creator royalties. This feature allows NFT creators to earn a percentage of sales whenever their NFTs are resold in the secondary market, ensuring ongoing compensation for their work. Additionally, some platforms may impose fees for actions like bid withdrawal to prevent non-serious bids, and less commonly, transfer fees for moving NFTs between wallets. Collectively, these various fees sustain the NFT ecosystem, incentivizing creators, supporting platform operations, and maintaining the integrity and efficiency of the blockchain network.

# P2E

"Play to Earn" (P2E) in the realm of NFTs represents a groundbreaking gaming model where players can earn tangible rewards, such as cryptocurrency or NFTs, through their in-game activities. These games are typically built on blockchain platforms, allowing for the creation of unique in-game assets like characters, equipment, or land as NFTs. The defining feature of P2E is that the rewards hold real-world value; players can trade their in-game earnings on various cryptocurrency exchanges or NFT marketplaces, effectively turning virtual success into real-world financial gains. This model also emphasizes the ownership and tradability of in-game assets, offering players genuine ownership verified through blockchain technology, and the flexibility to trade or sell these assets.

*Famous P2E games AXIE infinity and Cryptokittes*

There are some famous P2E games like "Axie Infinity" and "CryptoKitties", each offering unique gameplay and economic models. Axie Infinity, inspired by Pokémon, allows players to collect, breed, and battle digital creatures called "Axies," each an NFT with distinct characteristics. It operates on the Ethereum blockchain, using its own tokens - Axie Infinity Shards (AXS) and Smooth Love Potion (SLP) - for in-game transactions. This game exemplifies the "Play to Earn" model, where players can earn real-world value through in-game activities like battles and breeding, making it a significant contributor to the digital economy and online communities.

CryptoKitties, launched in 2017, was one of the first games to use blockchain technology for digital collectibles. Players in CryptoKitties can buy, collect, breed, and sell virtual cats, each represented as a unique NFT on the Ethereum blockchain. The game's breeding mechanism, where new, unique kittens are produced with varying traits, adds to its appeal. CryptoKitties gained fame for its massive popularity and for bringing widespread attention to the potential of NFTs in gaming, despite causing notable congestion on the Ethereum network. Both games have been instrumental in illustrating the use of blockchain for creating unique digital assets and fostering player-driven economies in the gaming world.

## Soulbound token and POAP

There are more fascinating ideas built on top of the NFT! Soulbound token and POAP(Proof Of Attendance Protocol) are one of them. Actually Vitalik Buterin wrote an interesting and descriptive post about what he thinks in his blogpost. Check out the article named "soul bound" for this if you want more details(I recommend reading his other blog posts as well, he is one of the smartest people in the crypto space and his articles are so elegant and well articulated about his vision).

Soulbound Tokens (SBTs) are proposed as non-transferable, non-financialized tokens on the blockchain. They are designed to represent personal credentials, memberships, or achievements, and are linked to an individual's digital identity. Unlike typical NFTs or cryptocurrencies, SBTs can't be sold or transferred, making them a permanent part of one's digital identity. This concept aims to enrich blockchain applications beyond financial transactions, fostering community, reputation, and identity in the digital space.

*POAP collected in 2021 and 2022. This gives you proof that you had actually attended events for POAP NFT that are each representing. Source: greywizard.eth*

POAP (Proof of Attendance Protocol) is a digital collectible that serves as a personal record of attendance at an event or participation in an activity. These tokens are unique, leveraging blockchain technology to verify authenticity and ownership. POAPs are used to commemorate experiences, and they can be collected and stored in a digital wallet, creating a decentralized and tamper-proof record of one's experiences and engagements in various events and activities. They have gained popularity in virtual events and communities, especially within the cryptocurrency and blockchain sectors.

## DAO

A Decentralized Autonomous Organization (DAO) is an innovative organizational structure that operates through smart contracts on a blockchain, primarily in the Ethereum ecosystem. At its core, a DAO is a collective governed by its members, who typically hold tokens granting voting rights. These tokens can be distributed based on contributions, investment, or other criteria set by the DAO. The rules of the organization, decision-making processes, and financial transactions are transparently coded into smart contracts, ensuring that all actions align with the agreed-upon protocols without central oversight. This model facilitates a level of democracy and transparency uncommon in traditional organizations, allowing for decentralized decision-making and direct stakeholder involvement in governance. DAOs are used for a variety of purposes, including managing collective investments, governing decentralized applications (dApps), and coordinating community-led initiatives, embodying the principles of decentralization inherent to blockchain technology.

## How the DAO works?

At the core of a DAO's mechanics are smart contracts, self-executing contracts with the terms of the agreement directly written into code, which run on a blockchain. These smart contracts are the building blocks of a DAO, dictating how the organization operates, including its rules for decision-making, fund management, and member interactions. Once deployed, these contracts operate autonomously, executing predefined operations when certain conditions are met. This automation minimizes the need for central authority or intermediaries, promoting a trustless environment where transactions and decisions are transparent and verifiable by all members.

Tokenomics play a crucial role in DAOs, often serving as a means to incentivize and regulate member participation and governance. In many DAOs, tokens are used to represent voting power, with the distribution of these tokens reflecting the stake each member has in the organization. These tokens can be earned, bought, or allocated based on various criteria, including initial funding, contributions to the DAO, or participation in specific tasks. The token-based voting mechanism is a key feature, ensuring that decisions regarding the DAO's direction, such as fund allocation, updates to the smart contract, or new project initiatives, are made democratically. This system ensures that the control of the DAO is distributed among its members, aligning with the principles of decentralization and collective governance. Moreover, the economic design of these tokens can also influence the behavior of members, aligning individual incentives with the collective goals of the DAO.

The structure and formation of a DAO are also critical components of its mechanics. Unlike traditional organizations that are established through legal frameworks and paperwork, a DAO is created by deploying its foundational smart contract to the blockchain. This contract not only outlines the rules and governance protocols but also defines the way in which new members can join and how the DAO interacts with external entities and contracts. The flexibility of this structure allows for a wide range of organizational models, from flat and fully democratic to more hierarchical and role-based, depending on the specific goals and governance style chosen by its creators. Additionally, since DAOs operate on blockchain networks, they inherit characteristics such as immutability, transparency, and security. However, this also brings challenges, such as ensuring the security and robustness of the smart contracts against potential vulnerabilities and adapting to the evolving regulatory landscape surrounding decentralized digital entities.

## Game theory and DAO

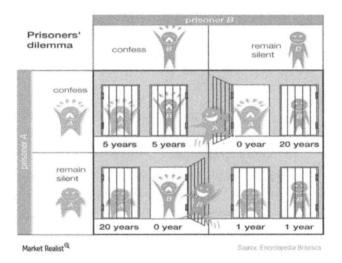

Market Realist

Source: Encyclopedia Britanica

*In the prisoners' dilemma, it is proved by the game theory that if they are not able to communicate beforehand, it is the best option to betray each other even if there is an optimal way which is to cooperate by both remaining silent(This is because one could get sentenced ridiculously a lot if the other betrays). DAO could solve this problem through its inherent characteristic of transparency.*

Game theory is an analytical framework used to understand strategic interactions among rational decision-makers, applicable across fields like economics, political science, and computer science. It revolves around players (decision-makers), their strategies, the resulting payoffs, and the available information. Game theory classifies scenarios as cooperative or non-cooperative, symmetric or asymmetric, and zero-sum or non-zero-sum, with decisions made either sequentially or simultaneously. Its wide-ranging applications include analyzing competitive business strategies, political negotiations, evolutionary biology, and algorithm design in computer science. By examining how individual actions impact others, game theory provides insights into the dynamics of decision-making in situations where outcomes depend on the choices of all involved parties.

The interplay between game theory and DAOs is pivotal in understanding how these innovative entities operate. Game theory, which studies strategic interactions among rational decision-makers, is crucial for designing effective DAOs. It offers insights into creating incentive structures that encourage behaviors beneficial to both individual members and the DAO collectively. This is particularly evident in the development of tokenomics and voting systems, where game theory ensures that participants are motivated to act in the organization's best interest.

In the realm of governance, game theory significantly influences the structuring of voting mechanisms and governance models within DAOs. It provides a framework for predicting member behavior in various voting scenarios, helping to design systems that address issues like majority dominance or voter indifference. This ensures that decision-making processes are representative and aligned with the collective welfare of the DAO. Moreover, game theory plays a critical role in conflict resolution, offering strategies to manage and mitigate potential disputes among members.

Collaborative decision-making is at the heart of DAOs, and game theory aids in understanding and fostering effective collaboration among diverse stakeholders. It helps in anticipating how participants interact, ensuring that the DAO's structure promotes positive interactions and outcomes where cooperation trumps competition. Game theory also assists in analyzing potential strategies and their consequences, allowing DAOs to make informed decisions and adapt to changing circumstances.

Lastly, game theory is fundamental in ensuring fairness and stability within DAOs. It guides the creation of environments that discourage negative behaviors like collusion while promoting fairness and equitable participation. The dynamic nature of DAOs, with evolving member strategies and interactions, makes game theory an indispensable tool. It not only helps in the initial design of DAOs but also in their ongoing management and adaptation to new challenges and opportunities. Thus, game theory is not just a theoretical framework; it's a practical guide that shapes the very foundation and functioning of DAOs.

## DAO in real life

### Gitcoin

*Gitcoin's grant sponsors open source projects that contribute to public goods. Source: gitcoin*

Gitcoin is a platform that fundamentally transforms the funding landscape for open-source software development, primarily within the Ethereum blockchain ecosystem. Launched in 2017, it is designed to financially support developers working on open-source projects that are vital to the digital infrastructure but often lack conventional funding channels. The platform operates by connecting project maintainers with developers, where maintainers can post bounties for specific tasks in their projects, and developers get compensated in cryptocurrency for completing these tasks.

## Allocation of funds using quadratic formula

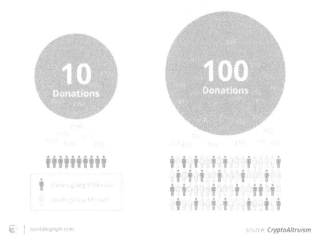

*"Quadratic funding" is a pure democratic way for
allocating funds for open source projects.*

A central feature of Gitcoin is its grants program, which provides an innovative funding mechanism for open-source projects. This is achieved through quadratic funding, a unique approach that prioritizes community support in the allocation of funds. In this system, the funding a project receives is determined not just by the total financial contributions it attracts but also by the number of individual contributors, thereby amplifying the influence of smaller, numerous donations over larger, singular contributions. This democratically-oriented funding model has been pivotal in promoting a wide range of projects, especially those offering public goods without clear monetization strategies.

Beyond bounties and grants, Gitcoin enhances community engagement through virtual hackathons, fostering innovation and collaboration. These hackathons connect developers with companies for problem-solving and technological development, with bounties offered for achieving specific goals. Additionally, Gitcoin incorporates peer-to-peer recognition features like digital kudos and tipping, allowing community members to appreciate each other's contributions. Reflecting the decentralized ethos it champions, Gitcoin is governed as a DAO, where key decisions about its future and operations are made collectively by its community of governance token holders. This governance structure further reinforces Gitcoin's commitment to community-driven development and decentralized decision-making.

## Olympus DAO

Olympus DAO is primarily known for its unique approach to creating a stable yet decentralized reserve currency. At the heart of Olympus DAO is the OHM token, which is distinct from typical stablecoins as its value isn't pegged to a fiat currency. Instead, OHM aims for a stable value backed by a diverse asset basket, with its operation governed by a DAO. This model empowers community members, who are token holders, to participate in decision-making processes.

The core mechanics of Olympus DAO revolve around innovative concepts like bonding, staking, and a dynamic rebase mechanism. Bonding allows users to buy OHM at a discount by trading in other crypto assets or liquidity provider tokens, while staking involves locking up OHM to earn rebase rewards, which increases the holder's OHM balance over time. The rebase mechanism is crucial for regulating OHM's supply, helping stabilize its market price by adjusting the circulating supply based on current market conditions.

Olympus DAO's approach, including its treasury management and liquidity strategies, positions it as an experimental yet influential player in the DeFi space. The treasury backs the value of OHM and contributes to overall system stability by holding a variety of assets. While this model offers significant potential rewards, particularly through staking, it also involves risks associated with market volatility and the experimental nature of DeFi projects.

## Ukraine DAO

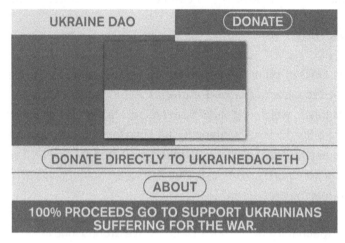

UKRAINE DAO

( DONATE )

( DONATE DIRECTLY TO UKRAINEDAO.ETH )

( ABOUT )

100% PROCEEDS GO TO SUPPORT UKRAINIANS
SUFFERING FOR THE WAR.

*People could fund charity with a relieving heart. Through the transparency of DAO, people could see where and how for the funds to be used.*

A Ukraine DAO is a DAO focused on addressing various needs and challenges within Ukraine. The potential objectives of a Ukraine DAO include humanitarian aid, such as collecting and distributing funds for victims of conflict or for rebuilding efforts; cultural preservation, aiming to safeguard Ukrainian art, history, and heritage; political activism, supporting democratic movements and free speech; and economic development, which might involve backing local startups or tech projects. The core characteristics of any DAO, including those centered on Ukraine, are decentralization, transparency, and democratic participation, where members propose and vote on initiatives, with all transactions and decisions recorded securely on the blockchain.

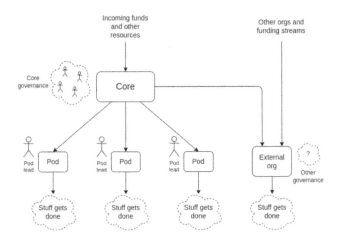

*Ukraine DAO workflow. Whereas the earlier DAOs are organized around providing infrastructure, the newer DAOs like Ukraine DAO are organized around performing various tasks around a particular theme. Source: vitalik.eth*

Unlike conventional DAOs, which centralize vast amounts of capital for distribution based on token-holder votes, Ukraine DAO adopts a distinctive approach by distributing its operations across numerous pods, each functioning with a high degree of independence. A governing layer retains the authority to establish new pods and potentially allocate funding, primarily to external entities supporting Ukraine thus far. Once operational, these pods are granted autonomy, managing resources independently while internally, they may have a hierarchical structure but strive to honor a principle of individual autonomy.

For such a decentralized structure to genuinely succeed, two critical factors are essential:

> **Pod Autonomy**: Ensuring pods have substantial independence, where they receive resources from the central entity but are subject to occasional reviews for alignment and performance. Outside of these evaluations, pods operate without direct oversight or commands from the central body.

**Diverse and Decentralized Governance**: Effective decentralization requires that the core governance system embraces broad and diverse participation. This does not necessitate a governance token but does call for inclusive engagement from a wide array of participants. While extensive participation often comes at the cost of efficiency, the autonomy granted to pods reduces the need for frequent central decisions, mitigating the impact of governance inefficiencies.

# Chapter 5

# Altcoins - Polygon, Worldcoin, Solana, Ripple, Dogecoin and Terra

Altcoins, short for "alternative coins," are cryptocurrencies that differ from the pioneering Bitcoin. They emerged as developers aimed to either improve upon Bitcoin's limitations or offer new capabilities. Technologically, altcoins vary in their consensus mechanisms, with many opting for alternatives to Bitcoin's Proof of Work (PoW), such as Proof of Stake (PoS) and others. They also focus on enhancing transaction speed and scalability – for instance, Litecoin processes blocks faster than Bitcoin. Additionally, some altcoins like Ethereum have introduced smart contracts as we have seen in Chapter 3, enabling the execution of agreements coded directly into the blockchain.

Altcoins serve diverse purposes and address various use cases. Some, like Litecoin and Bitcoin Cash, are created for general digital transactions, resembling digital money. Others, notably Ethereum, are developed to support decentralized applications (dApps) and smart contracts. Privacy-focused altcoins, such as Monero and Zcash, offer greater anonymity than Bitcoin. In terms of market dynamics, altcoins generally have lower market capitalization and higher volatility, making them both potentially riskier and more lucrative for investment. Their success often hinges on the strength of their developer communities and user adoption, and their legal and regulatory status varies across different jurisdictions, affecting their widespread use and acceptance.

The altcoin landscape is marked by its diversity and rapid evolution. They bring a range of functionalities, from faster transaction processing to the enablement of smart contracts and privacy enhancements, setting them apart from Bitcoin. While they present various risks like security vulnerabilities, liquidity issues, and questions about project viability, altcoins continue to be a significant and influential part of the broader cryptocurrency market. They are likely to keep shaping the digital currency and blockchain technology landscape, offering unique investment opportunities and technological advancements.

In this chapter, we will look at some interesting alt coin projects which are Polygon, Worldcoin, Solana, Ripple, Dogecoin and Terra-Luna. These projects each show off their own unique characteristics in this chaotic crypto space. It would be fun to know what is the philosophy of their creation, and their future roadmaps.

# Polygon - Dreaming a "Swiss army knife"

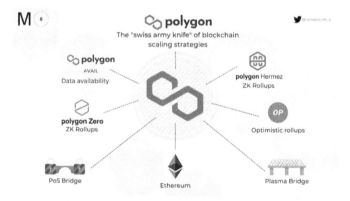

*Polygon's various scaling solutions. Polygon dreams to be the "swiss army knife" in crypto space.*

Polygon stands as a multifaceted platform designed to enhance Ethereum's scalability through a broad spectrum of solutions, aiming to provide faster and more cost-effective transaction processing. At its core, the Polygon Proof of Stake (PoS) Chain operates as a pivotal sidechain to Ethereum, utilizing a PoS consensus mechanism to facilitate quicker and less expensive transactions, while maintaining EVM compatibility for straightforward dApp deployment. Beyond the PoS Chain, Polygon diversifies its scalability solutions through the integration of zk-Rollups, with Polygon Hermez leveraging zero-knowledge proofs to batch multiple off-chain transactions into a single mainnet transaction, and Polygon Miden utilizing STARKs for privacy-preserving, scalable smart contract execution.

In its quest for privacy and enterprise applicability within the Ethereum ecosystem, Polygon introduced Nightfall, an Optimistic Rollup solution developed alongside Ernst & Young (EY) to enable private transactions. This initiative underscores Polygon's focus on catering to business needs for confidentiality and compliance on the blockchain. Additionally, Polygon Avail targets the enhancement of data availability for an array of blockchain architectures, facilitating the development of secure and transparent applications across its ecosystem. Polygon Edge further expands the platform's versatility, offering a framework for creating Ethereum-compatible blockchains with customizable features to suit varied project requirements, thereby promoting innovation and tailored blockchain solutions.

The Polygon SDK encapsulates the platform's vision for a multi-chain Ethereum ecosystem by providing a modular framework that supports the construction and connection of both secured and standalone chains. This strategic array of scaling solutions exemplifies Polygon's commitment to resolving the blockchain trilemma, balancing scalability, security, and decentralization. Through its comprehensive suite of technologies—from sidechains and Rollups to custom blockchain frameworks—Polygon is dreaming of a "Swiss army knife", preparing products and technologies for every possible circumstance.

# Meet Polygon's cutting edge products!

## Polygon Hermez

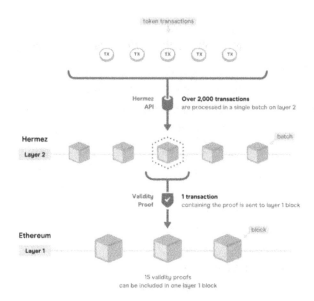

*Polygon Heremez flow diagram. It's underlying technology,*
*zkEVMs, take an initial state, process transactions, and output an updated state*
*along with a zero-knowledge proof.*
*Source: Polygon*

In order to understand how Polygon Heremez works, we should know what a zkEVM is. A zkEVM, or Zero-Knowledge Ethereum Virtual Machine, is a technology designed to enhance Ethereum's scalability and privacy without compromising compatibility with its existing ecosystem. By executing Ethereum transactions and smart contracts in a way that is identical to the original EVM, but with added benefits of scalability and privacy through the compression of transaction data into a single proof, the zkEVM can significantly increase transaction throughput and reduce costs. This technology maintains full compatibility with Ethereum's tools and smart contracts, promising a seamless transition to a more efficient and private blockchain infrastructure.

Polygon Hermez, initially known as Hermez Network, was the first decentralized Zero-Knowledge Rollup (ZK Rollup) on the Ethereum mainnet.

The transition to Polygon Hermez 2.0 marked a pivotal evolution towards a ZK implementation of the EVM, a milestone that hadn't been achieved before. Hermez 2.0 leverages cryptographic zero-knowledge technology to validate and finalize off-chain transaction computations rapidly, aiming to scale payments and transfers of ERC-20 tokens up to 2000 transactions per second (tps). This initiative reflects a concerted effort to reduce friction for users and dApps, employing a new suite of technologies and tools to recreate all EVM opcodes for transparent deployment of existing Ethereum smart contracts.

The merger between Polygon and Hermez into Polygon Hermez underscored a strategic foray into ZK scaling solutions, emphasizing the significance of zero-knowledge proofs (ZKPs) in enhancing blockchain scalability while ensuring security and privacy. This integration into the Polygon ecosystem, valued at 250M $MATIC tokens (around $250M at the time of the agreement), represents a first-of-its-kind full-blown merger between two blockchain networks. Polygon Hermez, incorporating the Hermez team and its technology, focuses on decentralization and the EVM-compatible solution, aiming to facilitate low-cost token transfers and improve Ethereum's scalability without compromising its security.

Polygon Hermez's architecture is open-source and decentralized, optimized for secure, low-cost, and usable token transfers on Ethereum. It offers more than a 90% reduction in transfer costs and a 133x throughput improvement, significantly enhancing the efficiency of token transfers and swaps. With a mission to create an inclusive and resilient payment network, Polygon Hermez employs zero-knowledge proof technology to ensure computational integrity and on-chain data availability. This solution not only promises to scale the Ethereum network efficiently but also to democratize access to financial services through reduced costs and improved throughput, all while maintaining a commitment to security and decentralization.

**Polygon Miden**

Polygon Miden is also a ZK-optimized rollup that aims to extend Ethereum's capabilities through client-side proving and a novel architecture designed for scalability, safety, and privacy. Unlike traditional rollups that prioritize

EVM compatibility, Miden focuses on ZK-friendliness, enabling features and applications that are challenging or impossible to implement on account-based systems like Ethereum. With its own STARK-based virtual machine (Miden VM), it facilitates the development of high-throughput and private applications, supporting developers to build using languages such as Rust and TypeScript while retaining Ethereum's security.

Miden introduces a unique transaction model that revolves around accounts and notes, allowing assets to be held and transferred in a manner distinct from Ethereum's approach. Accounts in Miden can hold assets and smart contract code, embracing account abstraction where all accounts are effectively smart contracts. This model enhances user experience by enabling safer wallets with functionalities like key rotation and social recovery. Moreover, Miden's architecture supports parallel transaction execution through an actor-based model, increasing the network's throughput. Notably, Miden utilizes a hybrid state model that combines UTXO and account-based features, facilitating privacy and scalability by allowing users to keep account data private and enabling concurrent transaction execution.

## Polygon ID

*Polygon ID verifies one's identity with zk-proofs without revealing one's privacy information. Source: Polygon*

Polygon ID is a digital identity solution developed by Polygon, utilizing blockchain technology to enable secure, private, and self-sovereign identity verification. It is grounded in the concept of decentralized identity, where individuals have complete control over their personal identity data, moving away from traditional centralized identity systems. Polygon ID operates using Decentralized Identifiers (DIDs) and verifiable credentials, both of which are key components in its infrastructure. DIDs allow users to have full control over their identity without relying on any centralized authority, while verifiable credentials enable the secure and verifiable exchange of personal claims using cryptographic methods. This approach not only enhances security and privacy but also ensures that users' identity data remains tamper-proof and immutable, thanks to blockchain integration.

This identity solution is designed to support both Web2 and Web3 applications, offering a blockchain-native system that is interoperable across multiple chains. It represents a shift towards self-sovereign identity models, where users have full control over their data, deciding what to share and with whom. The architecture of Polygon ID incorporates an Issuer Node for credential issuance, a Wallet SDK for developing identity wallets, and Verifier SDK for credential verification, aiming to facilitate a seamless and secure digital interaction environment.

The potential applications of Polygon ID are extensive, spanning various sectors such as finance, healthcare, online services, and government operations. In finance, it could revolutionize the KYC process, making it more efficient and secure. Healthcare could see improved patient identity management and secure access to medical records. For online services, Polygon ID offers a more robust alternative to traditional login methods, reducing dependency on passwords and enhancing security. Additionally, governments could leverage it to provide citizens with secure digital identities, simplifying their access to various services. Overall, Polygon ID's user-centric approach, where individuals control their identity data, combined with the security and immutability provided by blockchain technology, positions it as a significant advancement in the realm of digital identity management.

# Worldcoin - Sam Altman's dream of PoH

*The iris orb scanner for proof of personhood(left), Sam Altman who is the head of OpenAI, is also a co-founder of the WorldCoin(right)*

Worldcoin introduces a novel approach to digital identity and cryptocurrency. It centers around the World ID, a unique digital identity assigned to each individual through an iris scan using a specialized device called the Orb. This system aims to ensure that each person has only one World ID, thereby maintaining the integrity and uniqueness of each identity. Users interact with the Worldcoin ecosystem through the World App, which allows them to create an account and manage a digital wallet supporting various currencies, including Worldcoin tokens (WLD).

The project's inclusivity is one of its key features, targeting underserved communities by providing them with access to the digital economy. This is especially beneficial for individuals in regions with limited access to traditional identity verification methods. Worldcoin's proof of personhood protocol addresses the increasing need to differentiate real humans from bots and AI-generated identities in the digital world. However, the collection and use of biometric data for creating World IDs have raised significant privacy and data security concerns.

Worldcoin also speculatively suggests the potential for a decentralized cryptocurrency-based Universal Basic Income (UBI) system, which could offer a financial safety net globally. However, this remains a theoretical concept. The project aims for decentralized governance, but currently, certain aspects, including the control of smart contracts and data centers, remain centralized. This centralization, along with the challenges posed by diverse regulatory landscapes, significantly impacts the project's development and adoption prospects.

Security and reliability of the Orb, the project's hardware centerpiece, are crucial. Any security vulnerabilities could risk users' biometric information. The Worldcoin tokens, subject to market volatility, are distributed to encourage participation in the ecosystem, with a plan to expand the circulating supply as more users join. The project's ambitious blend of cryptocurrency and biometric technology aims to create a more inclusive and secure digital economy, but it faces significant challenges related to privacy, security, and regulatory compliance.

Sam Altman, co-founder of the cryptocurrency company Worldcoin and former president of startup accelerator Y Combinator, plays a significant role in the project. Worldcoin, founded in 2020 by Altman along with Max Novendstern and CEO Alex Blania, focuses on verifying a person's identity through iris scanning and aims to create a future universal basic income program. Altman's association with Worldcoin is seen as a positive influence by investors, and his role in the project is critical for its advancement. The recent fluctuations in Worldcoin's token price have been influenced by news about Altman's status at OpenAI, underscoring the impact of his involvement on the project's market performance.

## Worldcoin and ZKML

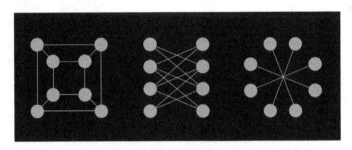

*ZKML opens a new chapter of ML with ultimate privacy technology. Source: worldcoin*

We have talked about zero-knowledge all day long and you might have also heard about what machine learning is in daily life, but what is the combination of those two? Zero-Knowledge Machine Learning (ZKML) integrates Zero-Knowledge Proofs (ZKPs) with machine learning to ensure privacy in ML processes. This integration is crucial for handling sensitive data or protecting the proprietary nature of ML models. However, this combination poses significant challenges, including computational complexity, scalability, and the need to balance privacy with utility. ZKML's applications span various areas: ensuring data privacy by training models on encrypted or private data without revealing the data itself, protecting ML model integrity to safeguard intellectual property, and enhancing privacy in federated learning by verifying computations without exposing individual data points.

Technically, ZKML employs methods like Homomorphic Encryption, allowing operations on encrypted data that yield encrypted results aligning with operations on plaintext. Another method is Secure Multi-party Computation, which enables joint computation over private inputs without revealing them. The advantages of ZKML are manifold, including enhanced privacy and trust in ML models, which is vital in sensitive sectors like healthcare and finance. It also aids in regulatory compliance. However, the field faces hurdles like the complexity and efficiency of ZKPs, the delicate balance between privacy and model performance, and adoption barriers due to the required expertise in both cryptography and machine learning.

The relationship between Worldcoin and machine learning, particularly ZKML, is rooted in Worldcoin's focus on privacy-preserving proof-of-personhood protocols. Worldcoin is specifically implementing zero-knowledge proofs in its WorldID system. This system allows individuals to cryptographically attest that they are unique human beings without revealing their identity and data to third parties. This is crucial in distinguishing humans from AI online while preserving privacy.

Worldcoin's application of ZKML is a forward-thinking initiative blending machine learning with blockchain technology and cryptography to create a secure, privacy-centric digital identity system. This innovative approach positions Worldcoin at the forefront of addressing modern challenges in digital identity verification and privacy in the blockchain and cryptocurrency domain.

## Solana - Insanely hot speed as a sun

Solana is an open-source blockchain project, launched in March 2020 by the Solana Foundation, designed to provide DeFi solutions. It stands out for its exceptional transaction processing capabilities, handling over 50,000 transactions per second (TPS). This performance is anchored by Solana's unique consensus mechanism, which combines Proof of History (PoH) with Proof of Stake (PoS), where PoH provides a way to verify the time between two events cryptographically, offering efficiency and reducing the need for the synchronized clocks used in other blockchain networks. Furthermore, Solana supports smart contract and dApp development, offering a robust platform for various blockchain-based applications.

The network's key features include its high throughput and scalability, which significantly surpasses that of older blockchain networks like Bitcoin and Ethereum. Solana's Proof of History innovation is pivotal to its speed, creating a historical record that expedites transaction and smart contract validation. The processing speed is 65,000 transactions per second (TPS) with low transaction costs. Additionally, the network maintains low transaction costs, which makes it attractive for a wide range of uses. Its capability to host dApps and NFT projects, combined with its energy-efficient consensus mechanism, positions Solana as a forward-looking player in the blockchain space.

The implications of Solana's technology are vast, particularly in the realm of DeFi and dApps. It challenges existing platforms with its high-speed, low-cost approach, potentially reshaping the blockchain ecosystem by attracting more developers and users. Solana's architecture enables real-time blockchain applications and broadens accessibility, paving the way for mainstream adoption of blockchain technology. Moreover, its energy efficiency aligns with the growing global focus on sustainable technology solutions, marking Solana as a key contributor to the evolution of blockchain technology.

## Solana, FTX and the infamous Sam Bankman-Fried

*Solana's R.I.P. right after the FTX crash*

The connection between Solana and FTX was significant due to Sam Bankman-Fried's role as an early supporter and investor through FTX and Alameda Research. The Solana Foundation's financial exposure to FTX was substantial, with assets worth approximately $183 million held on the exchange before its collapse. This included a mix of cash, FTT tokens, SRM tokens, and shares in FTX Trading LTD. The close association with Bankman-Fried and his entities bolstered Solana's growth but also tied its fortunes closely to the success and stability of FTX.

Following FTX's collapse, Solana's price plummeted, experiencing one of the most dramatic declines among major cryptocurrencies. The price of SOL fell more than 60% to a low point not seen since early 2021, with a significant portion of its market value erased. This stark downturn was a direct consequence of the lost confidence stemming from Solana's association with FTX, compounded by the financial turmoil and strategic vacuum left by FTX's bankruptcy. The market's reaction reflected a broader sentiment of mistrust towards projects closely linked to FTX, underscoring the extent of Solana's reliance on Bankman-Fried's backing.

The fallout from FTX's demise has had a profound and lingering impact on the Solana ecosystem, challenging its stability and future growth prospects. The sharp decline in SOL's price and the consequential outflow of developers and investors have raised questions about Solana's ability to sustain its operations and maintain its competitive edge as an "Ethereum killer." Despite these setbacks, Solana price started to rise sharply from the end of 2023 by increased user activity driven by Ethereum's high gas fees and Solana's enticing airdrops, particularly the Bonk memecoin, alongside the listing of its tokens on exchanges platform like OKX, enhancing its visibility and investor interest.

## Speed vs Centralization

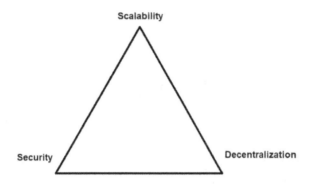

*Vitalik Buterins' trilemma of scalability in blockchain. It's essence is that one protocol cannot achieve all three(Scalability, Security and Decentralization) of those. For Solana, it chose it's position for having more strength in the scalability side.*

Solana distinguishes itself in the blockchain sector with its remarkable speed and throughput, managing over 50,000 transactions per second, thanks to its innovative Proof of History (PoH) consensus mechanism that complements Proof of Stake (PoS). This synergy not only facilitates rapid transaction processing but also ensures minimal fees, making it an attractive platform for high-volume or microtransaction applications. Its scalability and robust smart contract support enable the creation of complex decentralized applications, while its emphasis on energy efficiency through PoH and PoS aligns with the growing demand for sustainable technologies. Moreover, Solana's vibrant ecosystem and supportive community further amplify its appeal to developers.

However, Solana has some drawbacks, one of them is its network stability. The platform has experienced several instances of network outages and performance issues, raising concerns about its reliability. These outages, where transaction processing was significantly slowed or halted, are critical for a network that promotes itself on the basis of rapid transaction capabilities. Such incidents highlight the need for ongoing improvements in network robustness and resilience to maintain user trust and operational efficiency.

Centralization is another concern for Solana, stemming from the high hardware requirements necessary to run a validator node. This situation could potentially limit the number of nodes, leading to a more centralized network structure, which contradicts the fundamental principle of decentralization in blockchain technology. Additionally, the network faces security challenges, including potential vulnerabilities that might be exploited by attackers. While Solana is more energy-efficient compared to Proof of Work (PoW) systems, it still requires significant computational power, prompting concerns about its environmental impact.

The platform's scalability, while an advantage, also brings into focus the scalability trilemma in blockchain, suggesting a trade-off with decentralization or security. Solana's competition in the blockchain ecosystem, notably with established platforms like Ethereum, poses a challenge in attracting developers and projects to build a diverse and sustainable ecosystem. Lastly, the technical complexity of Solana, especially its Proof of History mechanism, although innovative, presents a steep learning curve for developers and users, which could hinder its broader adoption. These challenges underscore the need for continuous development and adaptation in Solana's approach to maintain its position in the rapidly evolving blockchain landscape.

# Ripple – Ultimate goal of global crypto payment

Ripple has emerged as a transformative solution in the realm of cross-border payments, challenging the traditional banking systems with its innovative blockchain technology. Its most notable contribution is the significant reduction in transaction times, bringing what typically takes several days down to just a few seconds. Alongside this efficiency, Ripple offers a substantial reduction in transaction costs. By enabling direct transfers between parties, Ripple eliminates the need for intermediaries, further streamlining the process and reducing fees. Its system's flexibility in handling various currencies, both fiat and digital, adds to its appeal, particularly for international businesses.

The security and transparency inherent in blockchain technology are at the core of Ripple's appeal. Transactions are not only faster but also more secure and transparent, allowing users to track their funds in real-time. This level of visibility and security is a considerable improvement over traditional banking systems.

Additionally, Ripple's scalability and its ability to handle a high volume of transactions make it a viable option for global financial institutions. Ripple's engagement with regulatory compliance and its partnerships with various financial institutions worldwide enhance its credibility and practical utility in real-world financial scenarios.

The interest in Ripple's cross-border payment system extends beyond financial institutions to individual users, primarily due to the benefits of lower fees and faster transaction times compared to traditional remittance methods. The ongoing legal and regulatory discussions surrounding Ripple and XRP are closely watched, as they are poised to influence the broader regulatory landscape for cryptocurrencies and digital assets. Ripple's success in this domain is not just a testament to its innovative technology but also an indication of the potential for blockchain to revolutionize global financial transactions.

## Ripple and the SEC, securities war

*There is a severe war going around between Ripple and the SEC about its securities issues. Gary Gensler, the chairman of the SEC, firmly states about Rippe as "Everything the SEC cares about, they lost".*

The legal battle between Ripple and the U.S. Securities and Exchange Commission (SEC), initiated in December 2020, is a pivotal case in the cryptocurrency industry. The SEC's lawsuit against Ripple Labs Inc. and its executives, CEO Brad Garlinghouse and co-founder Chris Larsen, alleges that they engaged in an unregistered securities offering, raising over $1.3 billion through XRP sales. The crux of the SEC's argument is the classification of XRP as a security under the "Howey Test," suggesting that investors bought XRP with the expectation of profits primarily from Ripple's efforts.

Ripple's defense challenges the SEC's classification, asserting that XRP should be regarded as a currency rather than a security and therefore not subject to the same regulations as stocks and bonds. They argue against the SEC's claim on two fronts: the lack of fair notice regarding the legal status of XRP and the delayed action by the SEC, which they claim suggests an implicit acceptance of XRP's legality. Ripple also draws comparisons between XRP and other major cryptocurrencies like Bitcoin and Ethereum, which the SEC does not classify as securities, arguing for similar treatment.

The implications of this lawsuit extend beyond Ripple and XRP, with significant consequences for the broader cryptocurrency market. The immediate aftermath of the lawsuit saw a notable impact on XRP's market position, with many exchanges delisting or halting its trade, causing a sharp decline in its price. The case is closely watched as it could set a precedent for how cryptocurrencies are regulated in the U.S., highlighting the ongoing issue of regulatory clarity in the crypto space.

In a landmark ruling on July 13, 2023, U.S. District Judge Analisa Torres decided that Ripple's sale of XRP tokens on public exchanges did not violate federal securities laws, marking a significant win for Ripple and the broader cryptocurrency industry. The ruling sent XRP's value soaring by 75%. However, the court also granted the SEC a partial victory by finding that Ripple's direct sales of XRP to sophisticated investors did violate securities laws. The complexity of this case and its implications have sparked discussions within the crypto industry and regulatory bodies about the need for clear legislation concerning digital assets.

This case has been closely watched as it could set a precedent for how cryptocurrencies are regulated in the United States. Despite Ripple's partial victory, legal experts suggest the ruling does not fully resolve the debate over when digital assets constitute securities under U.S. law. The outcome of this case and its impact on the regulatory landscape for cryptocurrencies remain subjects of significant interest and speculation within the crypto community and beyond.

## Ripple and CBDC

CBDC's combine attributes of traditional "fiat" currencies and cryptocurrencies — M2P

| Attribute | Central Bank Notes (Cash) | Central Bank Reserves | Deposits | CBDC | USDC (Stablecoin) | Xxxx (Stablecoin) | Bitcoin | Ether |
|---|---|---|---|---|---|---|---|---|
| | Traditional Fiat → | | | | | | ← Traditional Crypto | |
| Central Bank Liability | ✓ | ✓ | ✗ | ✓ | ✗ | ✗ | ✗ | ✗ |
| Legal Tender | ✓ | ✓ | ✗ | ✓ | ✗ | ✗ | ✗ | ✗ |
| Convertible at par to Reserves/bank notes | ✓ | ✓ | ✓ | ✓ | ◐ | ✗ | ✗ | ✗ |
| Interest bearing | ✗ | ✓ | ✓ | Depends | ✗ | ✗ | ✗ | ✗ |
| Electronic | ✗ | ✗ | ✓ | ✓ | ✓ | ✓ | ✓ | ✓ |
| Universally accessible (e.g., Anyone with digital signature can access) | ✓ | ✗ | ✓ | Depends | ✓ | ✓ | ✓ | ✓ |
| Token (Ownership tied to digital signature) or account-based (Ownership tied to identity) | Token | Account | Account | Depends | Token | Token | Token | Token |

✓ Fit   ✗ Not a fit   ◐ Partial Fit

*CBDC is a hybrid mixture of traditional fiat currency and crypto currency like Bitcoin and Ethereum. It is legal tender, backed by the central bank also leaving possibilities for universally accessible.*

What is a CBDC? Central Bank Digital Currencies (CBDCs) are a digital form of a country's fiat currency, issued and regulated by the central bank. Unlike decentralized cryptocurrencies, CBDCs are centralized and fully backed by the government, serving as a digital equivalent of physical banknotes and coins. The primary goals behind the creation of CBDCs include enhancing the efficiency and security of financial transactions, reducing the costs of managing physical cash, and potentially providing greater access to financial services for underserved populations.

CBDCs come in two main types: retail CBDCs, which are aimed at the general public for everyday transactions, and wholesale CBDCs, designed for financial institutions for more efficient interbank transactions. The technology behind CBDCs may vary, with some using blockchain or distributed ledger technology (DLT), depending on each country's specific needs and financial infrastructure. Central banks are responsible for regulating and securing CBDCs, ensuring the stability and integrity of this digital currency system.

The global interest in CBDCs is evident, with numerous countries exploring or actively developing their digital currencies through pilot programs. These initiatives reflect different economic contexts, priorities, and technological capabilities. The introduction of CBDCs could significantly impact current financial systems, potentially introducing new efficiencies but also disrupting existing banking and payment models. While sharing some technical similarities with cryptocurrencies, CBDCs differ fundamentally in their centralized control and regulatory framework, positioning them as a digital yet official form of a nation's currency.

## Ripple's ambitious vision for being a global payment

Ripple's expertise in blockchain technology positions it as a potential key player in the development of CBDCs. Recognized for its advanced capabilities in handling cross-border transactions, Ripple offers a valuable proposition for central banks exploring digital currencies. The company has proposed a specialized private ledger, adapted from its public XRP Ledger, tailored for central bank needs. This ledger promises high transaction throughput, robust scalability, and the security essential for national digital currencies, making it an attractive option for CBDC implementation.

Ripple's role in the CBDC landscape extends to providing technical and advisory support to central banks. The company is actively engaging in pilot projects and collaborations to demonstrate the feasibility and benefits of using its technology for CBDCs. A critical aspect of Ripple's offering is its focus on interoperability, advocating for a system where CBDCs can seamlessly interact with other digital currencies and existing payment infrastructures. This approach is vital for the widespread adoption and practical utility of CBDCs, potentially leading to more innovative and efficient global payment systems.

However, Ripple's path in the CBDC domain is not without challenges. The company's ongoing legal battle with the U.S. SEC over the classification of XRP poses a significant hurdle, potentially impacting its partnerships and credibility with central banks. Furthermore, Ripple faces stiff competition from other blockchain and fintech firms also aiming to collaborate with central banks on CBDC projects. Additionally, ensuring the highest standards of security and privacy in CBDC transactions is a critical concern for central banks, which will rigorously evaluate Ripple's technology before adoption. Thus, while Ripple's technology and expertise present a promising fit for CBDC development, its future role will be shaped by regulatory decisions, technological effectiveness, and the evolving requirements of the global financial ecosystem.

# Dogecoin - The most loved memecoin

## Who are you memecoin?

*Memes are like the living oasis of the internet.*

A meme, in the context of internet culture, is a piece of media, often humorous, which spreads rapidly online through social networks, forums, and other digital communication platforms. Typically, a meme involves an image, video, piece of text, or a combination thereof, which is copied and modified by users, with variations that reflect a particular cultural symbol or social idea. Memes are a form of digital content that can quickly become viral, reflecting contemporary cultural trends, social moods, or popular humor. Their rapid spread is facilitated by the ease with which they can be shared and adapted, making them a significant aspect of modern online communication and community-building. They often serve as a means of commentary on social, political, or cultural issues, encapsulating complex ideas in a simple and relatable format.

Meme coins are a distinctive class of cryptocurrencies, emerging primarily from the spirit of meme. The most iconic example is Dogecoin, which started off as a playful take on the "Doge" meme featuring a Shiba Inu dog. These cryptocurrencies are characterized by their light-hearted origins and are often not anchored in serious technology or business applications. The appeal of meme coins lies in their humor and the way they resonate with internet trends, setting them apart from more traditional, technology-driven cryptocurrencies.

The value and popularity of meme coins are largely influenced by social media dynamics and their respective online communities. Unlike conventional cryptocurrencies like Bitcoin or Ethereum, which have underlying technological foundations or practical applications, meme coins often lack intrinsic value or specific utility. Their market behavior is highly volatile, heavily swayed by social media trends, celebrity endorsements, and community sentiment. This makes them particularly susceptible to rapid and unpredictable price fluctuations, often driven more by speculation than by fundamental market factors.

| # | Category | Top Gainers | 1h | 24h | 7d | Market Capitalization |
|---|---|---|---|---|---|---|
| 8 | Centralized Exchange (CEX) | | 0.1% | -0.7% | 1.7% | $52,602,252,596 |
| 9 | NFT | | 0.9% | 6.8% | 8.0% | $26,082,387,498 |
| 10 | Liquid Staking Tokens | | 0.2% | -0.1% | -4.8% | $24,956,674,591 |
| 11 | Meme | | 0.2% | 4.8% | 3.7% | $24,394,082,188 |

*Meme coin sector takes the 11th largest position in the entire crypto space! Source: CoinGecko*

The market capitalization of meme coins stands at approximately $24.39 billion at the moment of December 2023. Memecoins hold significant market value largely due to their viral nature and the community-driven enthusiasm they generate. Often, these coins gain popularity through social media, celebrity endorsements, and internet trends, creating a snowball effect. This can lead to rapid increases in value, attracting investors looking for quick profits.

However, investors in meme coins need to be aware of their speculative nature and the risks involved. The accessibility and low price point of many meme coins attract a wide range of investors, including those less versed in the technical aspects of cryptocurrency. However, the lack of a solid underlying value or utility, combined with their susceptibility to hype and market sentiment, makes meme coins a risky investment choice. They are more suited for short-term speculative trading rather than long-term investment strategies, requiring caution and a clear understanding of their highly volatile nature.

# Coin with the cute Shiba Inu, Dogecoin

*The No.1 loved meme coin, DogeCoin.*

Dogecoin, a unique player in the cryptocurrency world, started as a humorous take on digital currencies in December 2013. It was created by Billy Markus and Jackson Palmer, drawing inspiration from the popular "Doge" meme featuring a Shiba Inu dog. Unlike other cryptocurrencies that often have a more serious and technical aura, Dogecoin was embraced for its light-heartedness, which played a significant role in building its large and enthusiastic community.

At its core, Dogecoin operates on blockchain technology, similar to other cryptocurrencies. This decentralized ledger system ensures secure and transparent recording of transactions across a network of computers. Dogecoin distinguishes itself with its mining mechanism, initially based on Luckycoin and Litecoin, using a proof-of-work system. Originally offering randomized mining rewards, it shifted to a fixed reward system in 2014. A key aspect of Dogecoin is its unlimited supply, a deliberate choice to encourage its use as a currency rather than an investment asset, leading to a lower price point compared to capped-supply cryptocurrencies like Bitcoin.

Dogecoin boasts faster transaction speeds and lower fees compared to many other cryptocurrencies, with a block time of about one minute. These features make it an attractive option for small transactions and online tipping, extending its utility beyond just an asset. The Dogecoin community further adds to its appeal, known for its charitable endeavors and a welcoming environment, which has significantly influenced its adoption and popularity.

## Elon Musk's no.1 loved meme coin

*Elon Musk's love of DogeCoin is famous. "One word:Doge", "I will eat a happy meal on tv if McDonalds accepts DogeCoin" are some famous tweets he had done in the past.*

Elon Musk, a CEO of Tesla and SpaceX, has played a significant role in influencing the popularity and market value of Dogecoin through his public endorsements, particularly on Twitter. His tweets about Dogecoin, often humorous and lighthearted, have not only brought widespread attention to the cryptocurrency but have also caused notable fluctuations in its market price. Musk's favorable comments about Dogecoin, which he has dubbed "the people's crypto," suggest a personal affinity for the meme-based digital currency. This has led to increased interest from a broader audience, extending beyond the traditional cryptocurrency community.

Musk's interactions with Dogecoin predominantly affect speculative trading, with his tweets often leading to immediate but short-term spikes in its value. This phenomenon underscores the sensitivity of cryptocurrency markets to the influence of high-profile individuals and the power of social media in shaping market dynamics. Speculation about potential future integrations of Dogecoin with Musk's business ventures is still going on. Overall, Musk's relationship with Dogecoin highlights the volatility and susceptibility to external influences that are characteristic of the cryptocurrency market.

# Terra - A meteoric rise and crash of algorithmic stablecoin

## Terra's ecosystem and applications

Terra was a cryptocurrency ecosystem featuring a unique approach to stablecoins and blockchain technology. At the heart of this system were two main components: Luna, the native token of the Terra blockchain, and TerraUSD (UST), an algorithmic stablecoin pegged to the US dollar. Terra's blockchain was designed to support various decentralized applications and to host a suite of stablecoins, with UST being the most prominent. The novelty of UST lay in its algorithmic nature, which aimed to maintain its value equal to one US dollar without being backed by physical reserves, as is common with traditional stablecoins.

The Terra ecosystem boasted a range of dApps that were pivotal in shaping its DeFi landscape. Anchor Protocol emerged as a standout, functioning as a savings and lending platform, offering high interest rates(20% annual) on UST deposits. This was achieved through a unique mechanism where interest rates were subsidized by LUNA's staking rewards, offering an attractive alternative to traditional finance options. Meanwhile, Mirror Protocol brought the concept of synthetic assets to Terra, enabling users to trade 'mirrored' versions of real-world assets like stocks. This allowed for decentralized exposure to traditional financial markets, broadening the scope and appeal of Terra's DeFi offerings.

In terms of governance and incentives, the Terra ecosystem was heavily centered around the LUNA token. Holders of LUNA were empowered with governance rights, allowing them to participate in key decision-making processes and influence the direction of the ecosystem. This democratic approach to governance ensured that the development and evolution of Terra's platform were community-driven. Additionally, the ecosystem incentivized users to stake their LUNA tokens, offering rewards for contributing to the network's security. This staking mechanism was not just a means to earn passive income but also played a critical role in underpinning the stability of Terra's stablecoins, including UST.

Terra's strategy for growth and sustainability also focused heavily on interoperability and collaboration. The platform was designed for seamless cross-chain interactions, enabling transactions and activities across different blockchain ecosystems. This interoperability was key in enhancing user experience and expanding Terra's utility beyond its native blockchain. Moreover, Terra actively pursued partnerships with other DeFi projects and platforms, integrating its stablecoins and dApps into broader ecosystems. These collaborations were essential in growing Terra's user base and strengthening its position in the competitive DeFi market.

# Algorithmic stablecoin, making money out of the thin air

**Terra's Algorithmic Market Module**

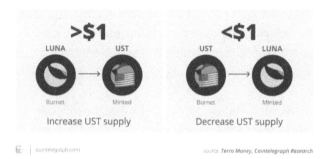

*source: Terra Money, Cointelegraph Research*

*When UST's value falls below $1 : people buy UST => burn UST and get the same value of LUNA => increase the UST value. Conversely, when UST is traded above $1 : LUNA holders burn LUNA => receive equivalent amounts of UST => decrease the UST value. In this system, arbitrageurs play a key role in ensuring the peg is maintained by exploiting price discrepancies between UST and its fiat peg.*

To prevent your confusion between terminologies, let me make it clear in the beginning. The Terra ecosystem revolved around two primary tokens: LUNA and TerraUSD (UST). LUNA, the native token, served several key functions within the Terra blockchain, including governance, staking, and importantly, regulating the stability of Terra's stablecoins like UST. UST, on the other hand, is an algorithmic stablecoin pegged to the US dollar, distinct from traditional stablecoins that are backed by tangible assets. The stability of UST is not maintained by physical reserves but through a sophisticated algorithmic process. While Terra is a whole system of making UST pegged to $1 by controlling the amount of Luna and UST.

The core mechanism that underpinned the Terra system was a minting and burning process involving both LUNA and UST. This process was designed to maintain UST's peg to the dollar. When UST's value dropped below $1, users could buy UST and burn it to mint an equivalent value of LUNA, thereby reducing UST's supply and pushing its price up. Conversely, when UST's price was above $1, users could burn LUNA to mint UST, increasing its supply and reducing its price. This mechanism was intended to be self-correcting, relying on arbitrage opportunities to keep UST's value aligned with the dollar. This process mimics exactly the traditional QE and QT by adjusting the money supply (in this case, UST) to influence its price stability, with LUNA acting as a lever to facilitate these adjustments.

The system's stability was theoretically ensured as long as there was faith in the Terra ecosystem and a sustained demand for LUNA. Arbitrageurs played a vital role by capitalizing on price discrepancies, helping to realign UST's value. Additionally, the process of burning LUNA to mint UST created seigniorage, the profit made from issuing currency, which was then reinvested into the Terra ecosystem, including a stability reserve. LUNA holders also contributed to the ecosystem's governance and security by staking their tokens.

## Fall of the Terra empire

*Do Kwon, was charged by a US federal grand jury with eight counts, is currently arrested in Montenegro waiting for a court decision about his extradition. Source: Wall Street Journal*

The collapse of TerraUSD (UST), an algorithmic stablecoin designed to maintain a peg to the US dollar, alongside its sister token LUNA, marked one of the most significant failures within the cryptocurrency space. Initially, the UST stablecoin began to wobble from its peg on May 7, 2022, plummeting to 35 cents by May 9, while LUNA's value dropped from $80 to mere cents by May 12. This dramatic collapse was precipitated by a series of large trades that exploited the relatively shallow liquidity of Curve pools, significantly impacting UST's stability.

Nansen, a blockchain analytics firm, identified that a small set of actors exploited these vulnerabilities by withdrawing UST funds from the Anchor protocol, bridging these funds to Ethereum, and swapping massive amounts of UST with other stablecoins within Curve's liquidity pools. This action undermined the stability of UST, leading to its depegging. Despite efforts by Terraform Labs and its supporters to restore the peg through substantial market interventions, including the Luna Foundation Guard (LFG) selling billions worth of Bitcoin to stabilize UST, these measures proved insufficient as the peg was lost, leading to a catastrophic sell-off.

On-chain data revealed significant UST inflows to Curve pools, indicating an intensifying battle between inflows and outflows around the time of the depegging event. Nansen's analysis highlighted that a handful of wallets were primarily responsible for the destabilizing flows, contributing to the hyperinflation of LUNA as users massively burned their UST in an attempt to exit, which ultimately led to the crash of both UST and LUNA. This event highlighted the risks associated with algorithmic stablecoins that rely on market mechanisms and arbitrage for stability, as opposed to being backed by tangible assets or overcollateralization.

The UST collapse serves as a cautionary tale about the inherent risks and complexities of algorithmic stablecoins. Unlike fiat-backed or overcollateralized stablecoins, which maintain their peg through reserves or excess collateral, UST relied on the dynamic interaction between it and LUNA to absorb price volatility. This incident has spurred discussions on the need for more robust mechanisms to ensure the stability of stablecoins and protect investors from similar events in the future.

Do Kwon and Terraform Labs are facing charges from the U.S. Securities and Exchange Commission (SEC) and U.S. prosecutors for orchestrating a multi-billion dollar crypto asset securities fraud centered around the algorithmic stablecoin TerraUSD (UST) and its sister token LUNA. The SEC's complaint accuses them of raising funds through the sale of interconnected crypto asset securities, including "mAssets" and UST, in unregistered transactions. They allegedly engaged in deceptive practices by promoting UST as a stable, yield-bearing asset through the Anchor

Protocol and making unfounded claims about the utility and stability of UST and LUNA. This led to UST's dramatic depegging from the dollar in May 2022, causing significant investor losses and a near-total collapse in the value of UST and LUNA.

Following the collapse, Do Kwon was indicted on charges including securities fraud, wire fraud, commodities fraud, and conspiracy, further intensifying legal actions against him. This criminal case, coupled with the SEC's civil charges, highlights the international legal pressures on Kwon, who was arrested in Montenegro after being a fugitive. The SEC's findings suggest that the stability of UST was artificially manipulated, marking the operation as a calculated fraud with potential unnamed collaborators involved. This situation has drawn attention to the regulatory challenges within the crypto industry, emphasizing the risks associated with algorithmic stablecoins and the need for clearer regulatory frameworks to protect investors.

# Chapter 6

# To infinity and beyond: Emerging technologies and future horizons

## RWA, the next Tsunami is approaching

*The head of the Black Rock, world's largest asset manager with $9.42 trillion in assets, Larry Fink states "the next generation for securities will be the tokenization of securities."*

The integration of Real-World Assets (RWA) with blockchain technology represents a significant shift in the financial sector, blending the tangible and digital worlds. RWAs, encompassing both physical assets like real estate and commodities, and intangible ones such as intellectual property and financial instruments, are being transformed through tokenization. This process involves converting these assets into digital tokens on a blockchain, offering enhanced liquidity, improved transparency, and democratized access to investment opportunities. The transformation brought about by blockchain in managing and trading these assets marks a pivotal step towards a more accessible and efficient asset management landscape.

The evolution of RWA within the blockchain space initially focused on digital-native assets like cryptocurrencies but soon expanded to encompass physical assets through tokenization. This began with real estate and gradually included other asset classes like commodities, art, and collectibles. The integration of these diverse assets onto blockchain platforms showcased the potential for fractional ownership, streamlined trading, and enhanced security in asset management. This evolution reflects not only technological advancement but also a growing focus on regulatory compliance and mainstream acceptance, making RWA more appealing to traditional financial institutions and broader investor bases.

Today, the RWA landscape in blockchain is both dynamic and diverse, with continuous developments, especially in the realm of DeFi. This integration is creating novel financial products and services, challenging traditional financial paradigms, and leading towards a more inclusive global economy. The ongoing evolution of RWAs on the blockchain underscores its role as a crucial element in the next generation of finance, highlighting a transition where digital innovation profoundly influences the management and perception of traditional assets.

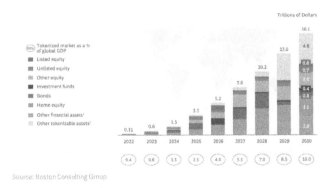

Source: Boston Consulting Group

*The tokenization of illiquid assets is estimated to be*
*a $16T business opportunity by 2030*

The integration of RWA into the blockchain is fundamentally anchored in the process of tokenization, which transforms physical and intangible assets into digital tokens. This process begins with the valuation and division of an asset into shares, each represented by a digital token on the blockchain. These tokens, governed by various standards like ERC-20 and ERC-721 on platforms such as Ethereum, enable the easy trading and management of assets, offering improved accessibility and liquidity.

Smart contracts are central to the management of RWAs in the blockchain, serving as self-executing contracts with terms encoded in the blockchain. They automate key aspects of asset management, from the issuance of tokens to the distribution of dividends, and enforce compliance with predefined rules and regulations. Despite their benefits in automating transactions and ensuring trustless interactions, smart contracts face challenges in legal recognition and adapting to complex regulatory environments. Innovations in this space focus on making smart contracts more adaptable and legally robust, addressing these challenges to ensure broader acceptance and implementation.

The blockchain ecosystem offers a variety of platforms well-suited for integrating real-world assets (RWAs) into the digital realm, each with its unique strengths. Ethereum stands out for its pioneering smart contract capabilities and vast developer network, making it a primary choice for RWA tokenization. Polkadot emphasizes interoperability, allowing for seamless cross-chain interactions essential for RWA liquidity. Tezos offers a stable and upgradable platform with a focus on secure and reliable smart contracts, whereas Algorand is recognized for its speed, scalability, and low transaction costs. Binance Smart Chain (BSC) provides an Ethereum-compatible environment with reduced fees, appealing for cost-effective RWA projects. Avalanche distinguishes itself with high throughput and customizable blockchains, ideal for diverse RWA applications. Flow targets digital collectibles and entertainment assets with its scalable, shard-free architecture. Lastly, Stellar is geared towards tokenizing financial assets, facilitating swift and economical cross-border transactions. Together, these blockchains form a robust foundation for the tokenization and management of RWAs, catering to various project needs from security and scalability to interoperability and cost efficiency.

## Tokenization, who are you exactly?

Tokenization refers to the process of converting rights to an asset into a digital token on a blockchain. Imagine a valuable painting or a real estate property; traditionally, owning and trading such assets involves cumbersome processes and paperwork. However, with tokenization, these assets can be represented as digital tokens, each embodying a fraction of the asset's value, much like shares in a company. These tokens can be bought, sold, and traded on digital platforms using blockchain technology, which ensures transparency, security, and immutability of transactions.

Tokenization in the cryptocurrency and blockchain space offers several significant benefits. Firstly, it greatly increases the liquidity of various assets. By transforming assets like real estate or fine art into tokenized formats, these assets become accessible to a broader audience, enhancing market liquidity and enabling fractional ownership. This process democratizes investment opportunities that were previously limited to high-net-worth individuals or institutional investors. Secondly, tokenization leads to faster and more cost-efficient transactions. It eliminates the need for traditional intermediaries in asset management, reducing transaction costs and processing times. Finally, tokenization enhances transparency and security. Since tokens are recorded on the blockchain, their provenance and transaction history are cryptographically verifiable, offering a level of reliability and authenticity unmatched by other digital assets.

The use cases of tokenization are diverse and transformative across various sectors. In real estate, tokenization enables fractional ownership, allowing investors to buy stakes in properties, similar to real estate investment trusts (REITs) or fractionalized NFTs. This approach significantly lowers the entry barriers to real estate investment. In asset management, tokenization allows for the fractionalization of assets, offering more flexible ownership and investment strategies. Contracts can be tokenized, enhancing the tracking, storage, and sharing of their associated terms and conditions. In the world of gaming and applications, tokenization increases user engagement by rewarding players with virtual assets, providing an entertaining and goal-oriented experience. Overall, the tokenization of assets opens up new possibilities for investment, ownership, and asset management, paving the way for more inclusive and efficient financial ecosystems.

## Tokenization process

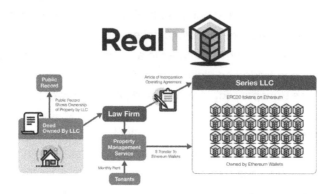

*RealT, tokenization process of leading real estate company*

1. **Asset Selection and Valuation**: The first step in tokenization is identifying and selecting an appropriate asset for tokenization. This could be a physical asset like real estate or art, or an intangible asset like equity in a company. The selected asset is then appraised to determine its current market value.

2. **Legal Framework and Compliance**: Before tokenizing the asset, it's crucial to establish a legal framework. This involves ensuring compliance with relevant laws and regulations, which can vary depending on the jurisdiction and the nature of the asset. Legal considerations might include property rights, securities laws, and anti-money laundering (AML) regulations.

3. **Token Design**: Once the legal groundwork is laid, the next step is to design the token. This involves deciding the type of token (e.g., utility, security, fungible, non-fungible) and its characteristics. The token design includes programming specific features into the token, such as rights, privileges, or terms associated with owning the token.

4. **Smart Contract Development**: Tokens are typically created and managed through smart contracts on a blockchain. These contracts govern the creation, distribution, and transfer of the tokens, ensuring compliance with the predefined rules.

5. **Token Issuance**: After developing the smart contracts, the next step is the actual issuance of the tokens. This can be done through various methods such as a private offering, public sale, or through a DeFi platform. The tokens are distributed to investors or buyers, representing their share or stake in the underlying asset.

6. **Token Management and Trading**: Once issued, these tokens can be managed, traded, or transferred on blockchain platforms. Token holders can buy, sell, or trade their tokens on various exchanges, depending on the liquidity and market demand for such tokens. The blockchain ledger records all transactions, providing transparency and security.

7. **Asset Management and Governance**: For some tokens, especially those representing a share in an asset or a stake in a project, there might be ongoing management or governance aspects. Token holders might have voting rights or a say in how the asset is managed, or they may receive dividends or other benefits.

8. **Redemption and Asset Liquidation**: Finally, there might be mechanisms for redeeming the tokens, either for a share of the underlying asset or for a cash equivalent. This could be triggered by certain events, like the sale of the asset, or could be available after a set period.

## Key players in the RWA space

The RWA sector within blockchain and cryptocurrency has seen remarkable growth, particularly in specific areas like lending, real estate, and treasuries and bonds. This growth signifies the increasing integration of traditional asset classes into the digital blockchain sphere, offering new investment and financial opportunities. This research was done due to December, 2023.

In the lending and private credit domain, Centrifuge and Clearpool have emerged as significant players. Centrifuge's active outstanding loans grew by 74%, reaching $155.7 million, while Clearpool saw a 966% increase in its loan balance, demonstrating the sector's rapid expansion and the growing appeal of blockchain-based financing solutions. This growth is part of the broader private credit market trend, which is estimated to be worth $1.5 trillion globally.

The real estate sector in RWA has also seen notable development, albeit at a slower pace compared to other sectors. RealT Tokens and Tangible have made significant strides in this area. RealT Tokens, holding a 49% market share in tokenized real estate, and Tangible, with its value locked in tokens increasing substantially, highlight the potential of blockchain in transforming real estate investment.

In the treasuries and bonds sector, Ondo Finance, Franklin Templeton, and Matrixdock are leading the charge. They collectively account for 85% of the tokenized Treasury and other bonds category. Additionally, Frigg.eco's focus on sustainable infrastructure bonds marks a move towards socially responsible investments, aligning with broader trends in finance.

Overall, the RWA sector's growth, marked by a 60% increase in market cap in 2023, reflects its burgeoning significance in the crypto space. This growth is especially pronounced in the lending sector, with a significant increase in outstanding loan values. The rise of tokenized US treasury bonds, with a 452% increase in market cap, further indicates a shift towards more secure and yield-bearing crypto assets. The evolution of RWAs suggests a promising trajectory for integrating traditional assets into the blockchain, potentially transforming investment landscapes and financial practices.

# Zero Knowledge, adding ultimate privacy

Since the word "Zero-Knowledge" has popped out a lot from the beginning of this book, you might be familiar with it by now.

Zero-knowledge proofs are a revolutionary concept in cryptography, allowing one party (the prover) to prove to another party (the verifier) that a certain statement is true, without revealing any information beyond the validity of the statement itself. This is akin to convincing someone that a secret exists without revealing the secret. These proofs are fundamental in blockchain and cryptocurrency technologies for enhancing privacy and security. They enable transactions or interactions where the relevant information (like the sender, receiver, and amount in a cryptocurrency transaction) is validated without actually disclosing the details. This not only preserves privacy but also adds a layer of security, as there's no sensitive information to intercept or misuse. The ingenious balance between information disclosure and secrecy makes zero-knowledge proofs a cornerstone in the development of secure and private digital systems.

Behind the Zero Knowledge there lies a heavy mathematical concept. In this section, we will only go through the surface and get a slight glimpse of the Zero Knowledge for the sake of our headache.

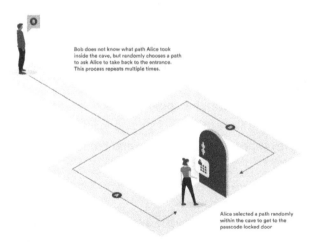

Bob does not know what path Alice took inside the cave, but randomly chooses a path to ask Alice to take back to the entrance. This process repeats multiple times.

Alice selected a path randomly within the cave to get to the passcode locked door

*Conceptual example of how a zero-knowledge proof works to prove knowledge about data without revealing the data to another party. Source: Chainlink*

To get a glimpse of what zero-knowledge really is, let's go through this famous "Alibaba Cave" example that shows the core part of it.

**The Setting:**

Imagine a circular cave with a magic door blocking the path halfway through. The cave has two entrances, A and B. There's a secret word that can open the magic door from either side.

**The Characters:**

- Alice (Prover): Alice claims she knows the secret word to open the magic door.
- Bob (Verifier): Bob wants proof that Alice really knows the secret word, but he doesn't want to learn the word himself.

**The Challenge:**

Alice wants to prove to Bob that she knows the secret word without actually telling him what it is.

**How It Works:**

- Alice goes into the cave and chooses either entrance A or B, but Bob doesn't see which one she chooses.
- Once Alice is inside, Bob stands at the entrance and shouts which way he wants her to come out from, A or B.
- If Alice really knows the secret word, she can use it to open the magic door and come out from the entrance Bob asked for, regardless of which side she initially chose.
- They repeat this process several times.

**The Logic:**

- If Alice does not know the secret word, she has a 50% chance of being on the right side Bob asks for each time. So, if they repeat the test enough times, the odds of her always being lucky enough to be on the right side by chance alone become extremely low.

- If Alice always comes out from the entrance Bob asks, he becomes more and more convinced that she does know the secret word.

**The Zero-Knowledge Part:**

At no point does Alice tell Bob the secret word, nor does Bob learn it through the process. He just becomes convinced that Alice knows it. This is the "zero-knowledge" part - Alice proves she knows the secret without revealing what it is.

# zk-SNARKs VS zk-STARKs

*Differences between zk-SNARKs and zk-STARKs. Source: horizon.io*

For cryptographic protocols which are rooted in zero-knowledge technology, there are two big players in the field. One is zk-SNARKs (Zero-Knowledge Succinct Non-Interactive ARguments of Knowledge) and the other is zk-STARKs (Zero-Knowledge Scalable Transparent ARguments of Knowledge). However, they diverge significantly in their implementation, applications, and implications for the future of decentralized systems. Let's find out their differences!

zk-SNARKs have been around for a longer time and are used in a variety of blockchain applications, most notably in Zcash. They allow a party to prove possession of specific information without revealing the information itself. The "succinct" aspect of zk-SNARKs means that the proofs are small in size and quick to verify. The "non-interactive" nature refers to the minimal interaction required between the prover and the verifier, usually involving only a single exchange of proof. A critical aspect of zk-SNARKs is the necessity of a "trusted setup," which involves creating cryptographic keys that are essential for verification and confidential transactions. While this offers efficiency and privacy, it also introduces potential security concerns, as someone with access to the initial setup parameters could potentially create false proofs. zk-SNARKs are known for their use in ensuring private transactions in cryptocurrencies like Zcash, where transaction details can be verified without revealing any sensitive information.

zk-STARKs, on the other hand, are a newer development in the realm of zero-knowledge proofs. They are known for their scalability and transparency. One key advantage of zk-STARKs is that they do not require a "trusted setup," meaning their security doesn't depend on the secrecy of some initial parameters, which is a potential vulnerability in zk-SNARKs. STARKs use cutting-edge cryptographic techniques that offer polylogarithmic verification resources and proof size, with minimal and post-quantum-secure assumptions. They allow for computations to be moved off-chain (to a single off-chain STARK prover) and then have their integrity verified on-chain by a STARK verifier. This approach significantly reduces blockchain verification costs while maintaining user privacy and computational integrity. However, one disadvantage of zk-STARKs is their larger proof size compared to zk-SNARKs, which can be a limitation in certain contexts.

In which circumstances, what type of system should we choose between zk-STARK or zk-SNARK? The choice between them should be based on the specific demands of the system. If the priority is efficiency and smaller proof sizes, zk-SNARKs might be more suitable. However, if transparency, no trusted setup, and quantum resistance are more critical, especially for large-scale systems, zk-STARKs would be the better option. It's important to note that both technologies are subject to ongoing research and development, which could influence their future applications and capabilities.

# Layer2 scaling solution

## Types of layer2 scaling solution

- **State Channels**: A state channel is a two-way communication pathway between participants that allows them to conduct transactions off-chain, with only the initial and final states being recorded on the blockchain, significantly reducing transaction costs and increasing speed.

- **Zero-Knowledge Rollups (zk-Rollups)**: They bundle multiple transactions into a single one, leveraging zero-knowledge proofs to ensure security. zk-Rollups store transaction data on-chain while computation is off-chain, offering increased transaction throughput and reduced gas fees.

- **Optimistic Rollups**: These assume all transactions are truthful, requiring proof only in case of disputes. They reduce on-chain computation, thereby increasing scalability and lowering transaction fees.

- **Sidechains**: Independent blockchains running parallel to the main chain, sidechains have their own consensus mechanisms and facilitate faster, cheaper transactions. It allows assets and data to be transferred between the two chains. However, their security depends on their own network, not the main chain.

- **Plasma**: Plasma in blockchain is a framework for building scalable applications through a network of child blockchains that report back to the main chain, enabling high-throughput, low-cost transactions by offloading the transaction processing from the main Ethereum blockchain.

There are five major areas in layer 2 scaling solution; State channels, zk-Rollups, Optimistic rollups, sidechains and plasma. The Layer 1 of popular blockchains often suffers from congestion, leading to slow transaction times and high fees, as every transaction is recorded on the main chain. Layer 2 solutions, such as rollups or state channels, operate on top of the base blockchain and handle transactions off the main chain. By processing and storing transaction data off-chain and only settling the final state on the main chain, these solutions significantly increase transaction throughput and reduce costs. This approach enables blockchains to scale effectively, accommodating a higher volume of transactions, which is crucial for widespread adoption in scenarios like microtransactions, DeFi applications, and general usage by a broader audience.

## State channels

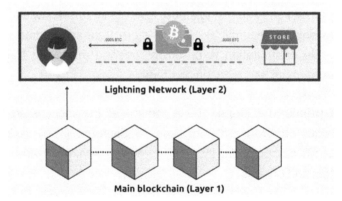

*Bitcoin Lightning Network, a representative example of payment channels, reduces the significant amount of resources due to recording only the final net fund moved between two parties to the main blockchain. Source: bitpay*

State channels are a two-way communication channel established between two parties. These channels allow multiple transactions to occur off-chain, reducing the computational load on the main blockchain. Only two transactions, typically the first and the last, are recorded on the blockchain. This mechanism enables parties to conduct multiple interactions, including financial transactions and status updates, in a private and efficient manner. The state channels utilize smart contracts to ensure that rules are strictly adhered to, and they rely on the underlying blockchain for security and finality of transactions

State channels offer several benefits, primarily enhancing scalability by processing transactions off-chain and thus reducing the load on the blockchain. This leads to faster transaction times and instant finality. They are cost-effective, as they incur minimal transaction fees, mainly during the opening and closing phases. Additionally, state channels provide increased privacy for transactions, as these occur off-chain and are not publicly recorded on the blockchain. This setup is particularly beneficial for applications requiring rapid, frequent transactions or microtransactions, offering a more efficient and private way of handling such interactions

Payment channels, being a specific type of state channel, are specialized state channels focused exclusively on monetary transactions. The Bitcoin Lightning Network is an exemplary implementation of a payment channel. In the Lightning Network, two parties can create a payment channel by locking up some Bitcoin in a multisig wallet, and then conduct numerous Bitcoin transactions between themselves off the main blockchain. These transactions adjust the balance between the two parties without needing to record each transaction on the Bitcoin blockchain, thereby significantly increasing speed and reducing transaction costs. The channel's final balance is eventually settled on the blockchain when the channel is closed.

## Zero-Knowledge Rollups

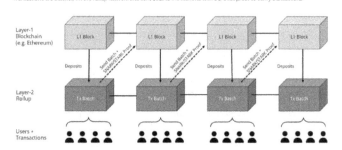

**ᴊ M E S S A R I**
**ZK Rollup Transaction Process**
Transactions are batched on the rollup network and sent back to the mainnet with a SNARK proof to verify transactions

*zk-Rollups solution is the most prominent scaling solution both handling scalability and privacy with zero knowledge proof. This system batches transactions in the layer2 side and sends the aggregated batch with the zk-proof to layer1 which makes layer1 to store only one transaction. Source: Messsari*

ZK-Rollups is the most prominent Layer 2 scaling solution up to December 2023, standing out due to their efficient data processing, robust security, and exceptional scalability. By processing transactions off-chain and submitting succinct proofs to the blockchain, they significantly reduce data load and gas costs on the main chain. This approach not only enhances transaction throughput but also ensures nearly on-par security with the underlying blockchain, thanks to the use of zero-knowledge proofs. Furthermore, zk-Rollups offer faster finality and improved privacy features compared to other Layer 2 options like Optimistic Rollups or State Channels. Their compatibility with the Ethereum ecosystem, supporting smart contracts and seamless integration with existing protocols, further underscores their effectiveness and appeal for widespread blockchain adoption.

So how does the zk-Rollups work under the hood? The core process begins with the aggregation of multiple transactions into a single batch, facilitated by an off-chain environment where a dedicated smart contract operates. This aggregation includes various transaction types, such as token transfers and smart contract interactions. Once aggregated, the computational processing of these transactions is carried out off-chain. This critical phase not only executes the transactional logic inherent to each individual transaction, resulting in an updated state, but also involves the generation of cryptographic proofs, which are central to the integrity and functionality of the zk-Rollup mechanism.

The essence of zk-Rollups lies in their use of zero-knowledge proofs, particularly SNARKs or STARKs. These cryptographic tools allow a party (the prover) to demonstrate the truth of a statement to another party (the verifier, in this case, the main blockchain) without revealing the underlying data or details of the computation. This ensures the validity of the entire batch of off-chain processed transactions. Following this, the rollup smart contract submits these zero-knowledge proofs and the updated state to the main blockchain. This submission is significantly more data-efficient compared to the entire set of original transactions. The main blockchain, upon receiving this information, conducts a verification process. This is designed to be computationally efficient, confirming the integrity of the off-chain computation as encapsulated by the zero-knowledge proof. Successful verification leads to the blockchain updating its state to reflect the new, consolidated state of the batched transactions, thereby settling multiple transactions in an efficient and secure manner.

## Optimistic Rollups

Optimistic Rollups are a Layer 2 scaling solution designed primarily for Ethereum, aiming to enhance its scalability by handling transactions off-chain. This method consolidates numerous off-chain transactions into a single batch and submits them to the Ethereum mainnet for verification. The process leverages calldata to compress and store transaction data efficiently on-chain, thus reducing costs. The state of these rollups, including accounts and balances, is organized in a Merkle tree format. Changes in this state are recorded on the Ethereum blockchain as new state roots, which the rollup operator submits following each batch of transactions. This mechanism significantly reduces the computational burden on Ethereum, leading to faster transaction processing and lower fees.

A key aspect of Optimistic Rollups is their use of fraud proofs. Unlike Zero-Knowledge Rollups that validate every transaction through off-chain proofs, Optimistic Rollups assume all transactions are valid unless challenged.

They provide a window during which transactions can be disputed, and if a transaction is contested, a fraud proof process is initiated. This process involves replaying the transaction on the Ethereum mainnet in a virtual machine-like environment to verify its validity. If the transaction is found to be invalid, the associated batch is reverted, ensuring the rollup's integrity.

Despite their advantages in improving scalability and reducing costs, Optimistic Rollups also have some drawbacks. One significant challenge is the delay experienced by users when withdrawing funds from layer two to the Ethereum mainnet, owing to the time required for external validators to check and challenge the Merkle roots. This delay is a trade-off for the increased scalability and reduced costs that Optimistic Rollups offer. Additionally, while they support smart contracts similarly to Ethereum, they also inherit complexities related to fraud proof validation.

## Sidechains

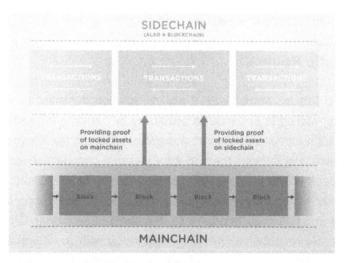

*Sidechain is literally a separate blockchain from it's related mainchain. Source: crypto.com*

A sidechain is a separate, independent blockchain linked to a main blockchain (also known as the mainchain or parent chain) through a mechanism known as a two-way peg. This connection enables the transfer of assets and data between the mainchain and the sidechain, allowing them to operate concurrently yet independently.

The concept of a sidechain extends beyond mere asset transfer. Each sidechain can have its own consensus protocol, block parameters, and security mechanisms, distinct from those of the mainchain. This independence allows for experimentation with different blockchain features and applications without impacting the mainchain's stability or security. For instance, sidechains can adopt faster block times or higher gas limits to facilitate quicker transaction processing and increased throughput, which is particularly beneficial for applications requiring high performance.

Sidechains also support general computation and can be compatible with the EVM, enabling them to execute smart contracts developed for Ethereum. This compatibility is a significant advantage for developers, as it allows them to deploy existing Ethereum dApps and smart contracts on these sidechains, often resulting in lower transaction costs and faster processing times compared to the main Ethereum network.

However, this independence and flexibility come with trade-offs. The most notable is the decentralization-security balance. Sidechains with more permissive block parameters might rely on fewer, more powerful nodes (validators), potentially compromising the degree of decentralization. Additionally, since each sidechain is responsible for its own security, they do not inherit the security properties of the mainchain.

Regarding their operation, sidechains utilize blockchain bridges for asset movement. When assets are transferred to a sidechain, they are typically locked in a smart contract on the mainchain, and an equivalent amount of the asset is issued on the sidechain. This process involves mechanisms like minting and burning tokens to maintain a consistent value across both chains. The use of smart contracts in this process automates and secures the movement of assets, but it also introduces potential risks if the smart contract code has vulnerabilities.

# Plasma chains

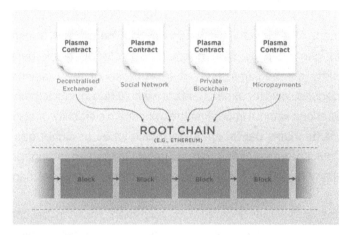

*Plasma is a framework for building scalable applications through a network of child blockchains that report back to the main chain. Source: crypto.com*

Plasma chains are a layer-2 scaling solution conceived by Vitalik Buterin and Joseph Poon. These chains operate as secondary, or "child," blockchains linked to the Ethereum "parent" blockchain. They are designed to offload a significant portion of transactional workload from the main Ethereum network, thereby facilitating higher transaction throughput and reducing congestion. By processing transactions off-chain and only periodically committing the state to the Ethereum mainnet, plasma chains significantly improve scalability and efficiency. This approach allows for the execution of a larger number of transactions per second, making Ethereum more suitable for a broader range of applications.

Plasma chains employ unique mechanisms like Merkle trees and fraud proofs to ensure the security and integrity of transactions. These chains independently validate transactions and generate cryptographic proofs, which are then submitted to the Ethereum mainnet. This method ensures that only valid transactions are recorded on the Ethereum blockchain. However, a significant challenge with plasma chains is data availability. Since most transaction data is stored with the chain operator and not on the mainnet, users must trust the operator for data access, particularly for creating fraud proofs. This can be a concern if the operator acts maliciously, potentially compromising the ability to challenge invalid transactions. To address such scenarios, a "mass exit" strategy is proposed, allowing users to withdraw funds simultaneously. Nevertheless, this solution has its limitations, including potential Ethereum network congestion and practical challenges in coordinating mass exits.

Plasma chain and sidechain seems very familiar by their design but there is a significant difference in terms of utility and security. Sidechains are independent blockchains running alongside a main chain like Ethereum, offering scalability through cheaper and numerous transactions. However, they carry a security risk due to their reliance on their own, potentially less robust, consensus mechanisms. Plasma chains, in contrast, offer greater security by publishing block roots to the Ethereum blockchain, enabling users to claim assets even if the Plasma chain fails. This higher security level aligns with the main Ethereum chain's security, but it limits Plasma chains in terms of operational complexity and the ability to perform complex operations, unlike the more flexible but less secure sidechains.

## Crypto Airdrops

*Free crypto falling from the skies, it's time for the*
*crypto airdrops! Source: forkast.news*

Did you know there are people who are making lucrative amounts of money through crypto airdrop? An airdrop in the cryptocurrency context refers to the distribution of digital assets, typically tokens or coins, to multiple wallet addresses for free. This practice is commonly employed by blockchain-based projects as a promotional strategy or as a method of decentralizing token ownership. Airdrops are often used by startups in the blockchain space to incentivize participation, increase the visibility of their project, or reward loyal community members. The recipients of these airdrops are usually selected based on certain criteria, such as holding an existing cryptocurrency (like Bitcoin or Ethereum) or being active within the blockchain community.

The process of an airdrop involves sending small amounts of the new cryptocurrency to the wallets of current holders of another established cryptocurrency. This is done automatically by the airdrop organizers and does not require any action from the recipients to claim the tokens. Airdrops are seen as a way to gain attention in the crowded cryptocurrency market, stimulate trading, and potentially increase the value of the new currency. However, they also carry risks, such as the potential for scams and the impact on token price volatility. As a result, participants are advised to exercise caution and conduct due diligence before engaging with airdrop opportunities.

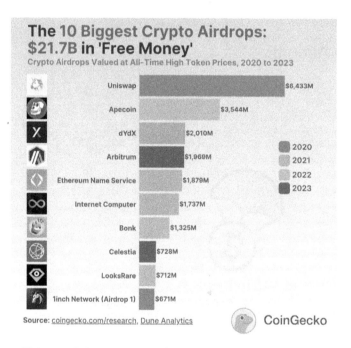

*Uniswap airdropped almost $6.5 billion dollars of UNI token. Followed by Uniswap, Apecoin and dYdX airdropped it's native token worth of $3.5B, $2B dollars respectively. Source: CoinGecko*

Uniswap's airdrop in September 2020 marked a significant milestone in the crypto airdrop landscape, distributing $6.43 billion worth of $UNI tokens at its peak value, highlighting the model's potential for widespread distribution and engagement within the DeFi community. This event, reminiscent of the DeFi Summer which happened in 2020 June from 2020 September, not only celebrated Uniswap's success but also paid homage to the origins of crypto airdrops, tracing back to 2014 with Auroracoin's distribution to Icelandic citizens. Following Uniswap, numerous projects have adopted the airdrop mechanism, aiming to incentivize protocol use and expand their user base, illustrating the enduring appeal and strategic value of airdrops in the crypto ecosystem.

In contrast, Apecoin and dYdX executed the second and third largest crypto airdrops, with values of $3.54 billion and $2.00 billion respectively, at their all-time high prices. Apecoin's airdrop in March 2022 rewarded Yuga Labs ecosystem participants handsomely, enabling recipients to essentially acquire a high-value NFT for free. Meanwhile, dYdX's airdrop strategy introduced a staggered release over five years, underscoring the varied approaches projects take to unlock value for their communities. Collectively, these airdrops contributed to 45.1% of the value amongst the top 50, demonstrating the significant financial impact and promotional leverage that well-executed airdrops can offer within the burgeoning crypto market.

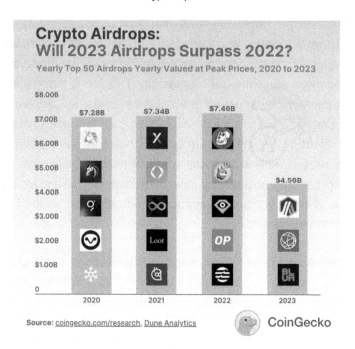

## Crypto Airdrops:
## Will 2023 Airdrops Surpass 2022?
Yearly Top 50 Airdrops Yearly Valued at Peak Prices, 2020 to 2023

Source: coingecko.com/research, Dune Analytics       CoinGecko

*Starting from 2020, 2022 was the peak year for total airdrop amount. In 2023, the amount has declined significantly to $4.5B. Source: CoinGecko*

The trend in crypto airdrops has seen fluctuating activity from 2020 through 2023, with a peak in 2021 when 18 out of the top 50 crypto airdrops occurred, contrasting with only 5 major airdrops in 2020 and a decrease to 14 and 13 in the subsequent years, respectively, likely due to the dampening effects of the crypto winter bear market. Despite this downturn, the total value of airdrops at their All-Time-High(ATH) prices showed slight growth from $7.28 billion in 2020 to $7.46 billion in 2022, with Bonk (BONK) notably breaking into the top 10 largest airdrops by reaching its ATH in December 2023. However, 2023 witnessed a decline in the total airdrop value to $4.56 billion, only 61.1% of the previous year's total, hinting at the nascent stage of many tokens airdropped during this period which have not yet seen a major bull market surge akin to those in previous years, especially during the notable bull markets of 2021 and the NFT boom in 2022.

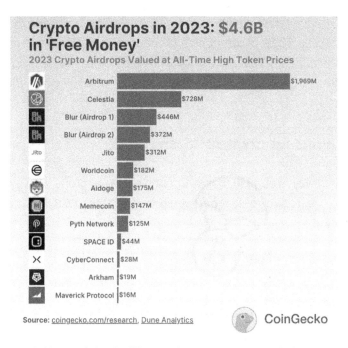

**Crypto Airdrops in 2023: $4.6B in 'Free Money'**
2023 Crypto Airdrops Valued at All-Time High Token Prices

| | |
|---|---|
| Arbitrum | $1,969M |
| Celestia | $728M |
| Blur (Airdrop 1) | $446M |
| Blur (Airdrop 2) | $372M |
| Jito | $312M |
| Worldcoin | $182M |
| Aidoge | $175M |
| Memecoin | $147M |
| Pyth Network | $125M |
| SPACE ID | $44M |
| CyberConnect | $28M |
| Arkham | $19M |
| Maverick Protocol | $16M |

Source: coingecko.com/research, Dune Analytics

CoinGecko

*Arbitrum, Celestia, Blur are the top most crypto airdrops that happened in 2023. Source: CoinGecko*

In 2023, the crypto airdrop scene witnessed significant activity with 13 airdrops making it to the top 50, cumulatively distributing $4.56 billion in tokens at their ATH prices. Leading the pack was Arbitrum (ARB), which executed the most substantial airdrop of the year on March 23, distributing $1.97 billion worth of $ARB, priced at its ATH of $1.69. This event marked a significant milestone, as the Arbitrum airdrop's value was nearly three times that of its closest rival, Optimism (OP), and was accompanied by a dramatic increase in the platform's Total Value Locked (TVL), soaring by 147.2% from the beginning of the year to its peak in May.

Following Arbitrum, Celestia (TIA) and Blur were noteworthy for their substantial contributions to the year's airdrop value. Celestia distributed $0.73 billion worth of $TIA, targeting a niche audience of developers, researchers, and active users in the Ethereum and Cosmos ecosystems, without resorting to the common 'farming' strategies of other airdrops. Blur, on the other hand, focused on rewarding users based on their engagement with its NFT aggregator platform, successfully conducting two airdrops in 2023, with the first distributing $0.45 billion worth of $BLUR and the second adding $0.19 billion at its ATH price. These three airdrops alone accounted for nearly 70% of the total value distributed in 2023, highlighting the strategic importance and financial impact of airdrops in the crypto industry.

## Precautions for crypto airdrops

It is an easy way of earning money through crypto-airdrops. However, there are some precautions before participating. Keep these 6 things mentioned in your mind!

1. **Verify Authenticity**: Research the project thoroughly. Check their official website, social media channels, and community feedback. Be wary of projects with little to no online presence or history.

2. **Beware of Scams**: Many airdrops are fronts for scams. Avoid airdrops that require private key disclosure, large deposits, or personal information beyond basic contact details.

3. **Use a Separate Wallet**: Create a dedicated wallet for airdrops. This protects your main assets from potential threats associated with unknown airdrops.

4. **Be Cautious with Links**: Don't click on unsolicited or suspicious links. Phishing scams often mimic airdrops to steal information or funds.

5. **Understand Tax Implications**: Be aware that receiving airdrops may have tax implications based on your country's regulations.

6. **Stay Updated**: Regularly follow crypto news sources to stay informed about legitimate airdrops and known scams.

# Bitcoin ETF

The approval of Bitcoin ETFs was a watershed moment for the cryptocurrency space, acting as a crucial bridge between traditional finance and the rapidly evolving digital asset sector. It represents a significant step towards the legitimization and mainstream acceptance of Bitcoin, enabling institutional and retail investors alike to gain exposure to Bitcoin without the complexities of direct ownership or the challenges of navigating cryptocurrency exchanges.

This regulatory milestone enhances market accessibility, potentially attracting a surge of institutional capital into Bitcoin, which could drive up its price and volatility. Furthermore, by providing a regulated, transparent, and familiar investment vehicle, Bitcoin ETFs could reduce barriers to entry, increase liquidity, and foster wider adoption of cryptocurrencies, thereby influencing the broader financial ecosystem and signaling a new era of crypto integration into conventional investment portfolios.

## What is an ETF?

An Exchange-Traded Fund (ETF) is a type of investment fund that is traded on stock exchanges, much like stocks. It aims to track the performance of a specific index, commodity, bonds, or a basket of assets. Unlike mutual funds, which are only traded at the end of the trading day, ETFs can be bought and sold throughout the trading day at market prices. This trading flexibility is one of the key features that distinguish ETFs from traditional mutual funds. ETFs are managed by financial institutions that hold the underlying assets, and investors buy shares in the ETF itself, not the assets it tracks. This structure allows for the creation and redemption of shares directly with institutional investors in large blocks known as "creation units," contributing to the ETF's liquidity and price accuracy relative to the underlying assets.

ETFs offer several advantages, including the ability to trade like a stock, which provides high liquidity and the possibility of intraday trading. They also offer the diversification of a mutual fund, as a single ETF can hold a wide array of assets across different sectors or geographies. Additionally, ETFs are known for their lower expense ratios compared to mutual funds, though investors need to consider brokerage commissions. The transparency of ETFs is another benefit, as they regularly disclose their holdings, giving investors clear visibility into what they own. Moreover, ETFs are generally more tax-efficient than mutual funds due to their unique structure, which can lead to fewer capital gains tax liabilities.

## Why is the Bitcoin ETF's approval so important?

The approval of Bitcoin ETFs has been a contentious and significant issue in the cryptocurrency industry, primarily because it represents a bridge between traditional financial markets and the evolving digital asset ecosystem. The U.S. Securities and Exchange Commission's (SEC) approval of spot Bitcoin ETFs, after years of rejections and regulatory skepticism, marked a watershed moment, underpinned by a federal appeals court reversing the SEC's decision to block such ETFs. This legal victory for proponents of Bitcoin ETFs, like Grayscale Investments, signaled potential for increased institutional adoption, as it made Bitcoin accessible through traditional investment channels without direct ownership of the cryptocurrency. The approval suggests a shift in regulatory stance and opens the door for significant capital inflow, with market experts anticipating that Bitcoin ETFs could attract billions of dollars in the first few years, potentially influencing Bitcoin's price and market dynamics significantly.

This move towards integrating Bitcoin into conventional financial products like ETFs is seen as a major step toward legitimizing and stabilizing the cryptocurrency market. ETFs are popular investment vehicles that offer the advantages of stocks combined with the diversified risk of mutual funds, and their entry into the Bitcoin space is expected to bring new investor cohorts from traditional finance, enhancing market transparency and liquidity. Financial analysts predict a substantial impact on the digital assets market, with expectations of long-term capital inflow and a considerable increase in Bitcoin's market value. This development is particularly significant given the vast assets managed by registered investment advisers, brokers-dealers, and banks, which have previously been hesitant or unable to engage with crypto assets directly. The approval of Bitcoin ETFs could thus catalyze a broader acceptance and integration of cryptocurrency within the mainstream financial system.

*Bitcoin ETFs approval made traditional investors get more*
*easy access for investing Bitcoin, leading it's price pump.*
*Source: cryptonews*

## Bitcoin price pump

The approval of Bitcoin ETFs has had a notable impact on Bitcoin's price, bringing a renewed sense of optimism to the cryptocurrency market. The SEC approval of 11 applications for spot Bitcoin ETFs, including from major financial institutions like BlackRock and Fidelity, has signaled a pivotal moment for institutional investment in Bitcoin. This regulatory milestone has led to a surge in Bitcoin's price, pushing it near 21-month highs, as it opens the door for substantial institutional capital inflows into the digital asset. Such a development is expected to drive greater demand for Bitcoin, as it enables both retail and institutional investors to gain exposure to Bitcoin through traditional brokerage accounts, simplifying the investment process and potentially leading to significant price escalation.

Experts predict that the influx of institutional capital could trigger rapid price increases for Bitcoin, with some forecasts suggesting the potential for the cryptocurrency to reach as high as $1 million. This optimism is rooted in the belief that Bitcoin's limited supply, combined with substantial capital inflow, will lead to dramatic price increases. Additionally, the approval of Bitcoin ETFs is seen as a game-changer, providing a regulated path for institutional investors to enter the market. The combination of limited supply, institutional interest, and favorable macroeconomic conditions presents a compelling case for Bitcoin's continued price ascent. The approval of Bitcoin ETFs not only marks a significant shift towards mainstream financial acceptance of cryptocurrencies but also sets the stage for potentially transformative growth in the crypto ecosystem.

# Reference

## Chapter 1

https://www.youtube.com/watch?v=yJfgWh1U-5w&ab_channel=BeSmart

https://seekingalpha.com/article/4384862-money-printing-2020-vs-2008

https://nakamoto.com/the-cypherpunks/

https://www.tesocollegealoet.sc.ug/news/hyperinflation-in-zimbabwe/

https://abcnews.go.com/Business/fed-decide-rate-hike-testing-optimism-soft-
landing/story?id=103286884

https://insights.som.yale.edu/insights/how-the-nixon-shock-remade-the-world-
economy

https://www.bbc.com/news/business-41021422

## Chapter 2

https://university.alchemy.com/course/ethereum

https://en.wikipedia.org/wiki/Symmetric-key_algorithm

https://ethereum.org/sl/developers/tutorials/merkle-proofs-for-offline-data-integrity/

https://keshavsps.blogspot.com/2017/11/bit-vs-byte.html

https://web.stanford.edu/class/cs101/bits-bytes.html

https://thresh0ld.com/bitcoin-utxo-what-is-it/

https://learnmeabitcoin.com/technical/script

https://ethereum.org/en/whitepaper/

https://www.horizen.io/academy/blockchain-protocols/

https://paymentandbanking.com/what-is-bitcoin-mining-and-how-does-it-actually-
work/

https://tangem.com/en/blog/post/what-are-hard-forks-and-soft-forks/

## Chapter 3

https://ethereum.org/en/whitepaper/

https://ethereum.github.io/yellowpaper/paper

https://coinsbench.com/a-comprehensive-guide-to-the-create2-opcode-in-solidity-7c6d40e3f1af

https://github.com/ethereum/solidity/blob/develop/docs/introduction-to-smart-contracts.rst

https://cointelegraph.com/learn/what-is-mev-ethereums-invisible-tax

https://docs.alchemy.com/docs/patricia-merkle-tries

# Chapter 4

https://www.entrepreneur.com/money-finance/3-lessons-from-the-summer-defi-boom/358661

https://www.bsc.news/post/uniswap-project-insight-a-pioneer-in-the-decentralised-amm-space

https://www.statista.com/statistics/1235263/nft-art-monthly-sales-value/

https://coinmarketcap.com/academy/article/what-is-blur-features-and-tokenomics

https://docs.opensea.io/docs/metadata-standards

https://blog.kryll.io/poap-nft-rewards-your-presence/

https://www.pymnts.com/cryptocurrency/2022/how-do-stablecoin-issuers-make-money/

https://finematics.com/is-yield-farming-dead/

https://www.theblock.co/data/decentralized-finance/derivatives

https://vc-courses.anu.edu.au/primer/game_theory_herschell/

https://vitalik.eth.limo/general/2022/09/20/daos.html

# Chapter 5

https://polygon.technology/blog/polygon-2-0-protocol-vision-and-architecture

https://worldcoin.org/blog/engineering/intro-to-zkml

https://m2pfintech.com/blog/central-bank-digital-currency-cbdc-101-a-primer/

https://medium.com/momentum6/polygon-overview-layer-2-or-sidechain-a888104f5ffc

https://docs.polygon.technology/zkEVM/

https://chain.link/education-hub/zkevm

# Chapter 6

https://www.galaxy.com/insights/research/overview-of-on-chain-rwas/

https://tokeninsight.com/en/news/rwa-sector-grows-fast-with-market-cap-increases-60-in-2023-tokeninsight-report-shows

https://www.gemini.com/cryptopedia/what-is-tokenization-definition-crypto-token

https://realt.co/introducing-realt-tokenizing-real-estate-on-ethereum/

https://ethereum.org/en/developers/docs/scaling/

https://blog.cwallet.com/state-channels-explained/

https://academy.binance.com/en/articles/what-are-zk-rollups-the-layer-2-scalability-technique

https://www.alchemy.com/overviews/optimistic-rollups/

https://docs.plasma.group/en/latest/src/plasma/sidechains.html

https://www.coingecko.com/learn/new-crypto-airdrop-rewards

https://www.investing.com/analysis/the-top-10-ethereum-token-airdrops-rumored-for-2022-200612882

https://www.coingecko.com/research/publications/biggest-crypto-airdrops

www.ingramcontent.com/pod-product-compliance
Lightning Source LLC
Chambersburg PA
CBHW051238050326
40689CB00007B/968